AIDAN NICHOLS O.P.

CRITICISING THE CRITICS

Catholic Apologias for Today

FAMILY PUBLICATIONS

An earlier version of Chapter Six first appeared in
Proclaiming the Gospel of Life, published by CTS.

Front Cover: Pope Leo X by Raphael Sanzio (detail)
© Photo SCALA, Florence

ISBN 978 1 907380 04 4

published by
Family Publications, Denis Riches House,
66, Sandford Lane, Oxford, OX1 5RP, UK
www.familypublications.co.uk

Printed in England by
Cromwell Press Group, Trowbridge, Wilts.

Contents

PREFACE

Catholicism – and the Catholic Church at each stage of her history – is always well supplied with critics. When the Church is not all she should be – morally, intellectually, pastorally, aesthetically – such critics will often have useful points to make. And whenever, we may ask, *is* she all that she should be, short of the Parousia?

Critics essentially both benign and right-thinking are not, however, the only kind of critics that exist. Others, far from benign, may well be intemperate, even irrational, in their passions. Others again, possibly benign, offer their criticisms – whether from without or within – owing to a failure to grasp certain aspects of Catholic truth. This last category includes the critics this book has it in mind to criticise in turn.

I offer here a series of apologias for different facets of the truth of faith and morals held by the Church. The apologias are, it may be said, ill-assorted, and I can hardly deny the claim. It is part and parcel of the present conjuncture that intellectual assaults come from very different quarters at one and the same time. Those considered here are by no means all there are, but they are among those I personally have encountered and sought to answer. The audiences have been very varied – the Oxford Newman Society (Chapter 1); the annual conference of *Kirkelig*

Fornyelse, the umbrella organisation of catholicising movements in Christianity in Norway (Chapter 2); the Walsingham Retreat of the (Anglican) Federation of Catholic Priests (Chapter 3); a summer school of (what became) the International Institute for Culture at Eichstätt in Bavaria (Chapter 4); the international bi-lateral dialogue of the Catholic Church with the Disciples of Christ at Klosterneuburg in Austria (Chapter 5); a day of recollection of the Association of Priests for the Gospel of Life (Chapter 6); a conference to the young clergy of the Giffard Society (Chapter 7); the Craigmyle lecture of the Catholic Union (Chapter 8).

With the partial exception of the opening chapter, I have not spent a great deal of time in describing the positions I oppose. I have preferred to concentrate on the positive exposition of Catholic truth. Each chapter might be described as a quid pro quo, an offering appropriate, in its own way, to each of the categories of person involved. Readers of *The Lord of the Rings* may recall how, after his 'eleventy-first' birthday party, Bilbo Baggins left a set of carefully selected and labelled packages for various miscreant family members and friends. Clearing out the hobbit-hole of my room, these essays serve *mutatis mutandis* a like end.

Finally, I would like to thank Fr Vivian Boland, of the Order of Preachers, for contributing a number of helpful suggestions and corrections.

Blackfriars, Cambridge
Memorial day of St Francis Xavier, 2009

Chapter One

FOR MODERNISTS:
MODERNISM A CENTURY ON

Preamble

Historic Modernism is a phenomenon of the late nineteenth and early twentieth centuries, though later in the twentieth century it acquired a certain after-life. If we ask, 'What was Modernism?', the most coherent reply is furnished by the 1907 encyclical of Pope St Pius X, known in the usual curial style from its opening words, *Pascendi dominici gregis*: 'Feeding the Lord's Flock'. As we shall see, Pius X makes plain his awareness that in the writing, or editing, of this encyclical he was constructing an identikit picture which, in its completeness, fitted no one individual. Since I am not one of those who, for this reason, regard the Modernism identified by Pius as an Aunt Sally, straw man, or bogey, ideological projection, or at any rate phenomenon with a low reality-quotient, I am happy to define the Modernist *Weltanschauung* in broadly – though not, I hope, uncritically – the terms the encyclical suggests. It will be helpful, then, in the first part of this essay to present the main lines of Pius X's encyclical *Pascendi dominici gregis* which, like many writing or speaking on this topic, I will refer to for brevity's sake as simply *Pascendi*.

'Pascendi': introducing Modernism

The connexion between the title and the body of the document is simple enough. Feeding the Lord's flock as pope, that is, acting as supreme pastor in the Church, entails first and foremost, so claims the preamble, guarding with 'the greatest vigilance' the apostolic 'deposit', the faith committed to the 'saints', the heads of the new community.[1] The situation, explains Pius X, is grave. Laymen and clergy who lack the protection of sound philosophy and theology are setting themselves up as would-be reformers of the Church and her faith. Typically, they are men of erudition and strict moral probity. But they also, in his words, 'double the parts of rationalist and Catholic, and this so craftily that they easily lead the unwary into error'.[2] Although their contributions lack order, system and unity, this, says the pope, in the historically most dubious claim of the encyclical, is a feint, a pretence. They know perfectly well at what they are aiming which is a total 'make-over' (in our contemporary parlance) of revelation as hitherto understood. They present themselves under diverse hats, specifically, recounts the pope, as philosopher, believer, theologian, historian, critic, apologist, and reformer.

Pascendi will seek to show that, when their contributions in these various roles are connected up, a system of thought emerges. A series of principles with wide-ranging consequences stands forth. The rest of the encyclical pursues this analysis, under the seven headings – from philosopher to Church reformer – by which Pius identifies the various formalities in which Modernist writers view the substance of the faith.[3]

The Modernist as philosopher

The problematic quality of Modernist writing begins with its philosophical convictions, or lack of them. Modernism is characterised by metaphysical agnosticism; it regards human reason as confined to examination of phenomena, and denies its capacity to move from sense experience to an affirmation of the existence of God. Modernists draw the inference that, in the pope's words, 'God can never be the direct object of science [i.e. of natural human knowledge of the cosmos], and that, as regards history, he must not be considered as an historical subject [i.e. a real, though transcendent, initiator of historical action]'.[4] The consequence is that natural theology flies out of the window, and along with it any attempt to present a reasonable case for the occurrence of a revelation of God within history: what the pope calls the 'motives of credibility of external revelation'.

The phrase 'motives of credibility' – meaning: reasons for believing – is classic in Catholic teaching; by contrast, the qualification of revelation as 'external' is an innovation of the pope's, the purpose of which we shall see shortly. Modernists – probably the Anglo-Irish Jesuit George Tyrrell was in mind here – decry as 'intellectualism' the attempt to show the rationality of belief in God's existence and perfection, and the reasonableness of the act of faith in an historic revelation climaxing in Jesus Christ.[5] Their denial of the value of apologetics can also be called, says the pope, an assertion – an assertion, namely, of the necessarily atheistic character of both science and history.

The Modernist as believer

How, then, do Modernists, who after all are practising Catholic Christians, propose to commend religion – to explain it in positive terms? They do so, says Pius, by appeal, in effect, to a principle of 'vital immanence' – words which to some readers immediately summoned up the name of the French 'philosopher of action', Maurice Blondel. If natural theology is non-viable, and no arguments for external revelation in history can be proposed, then the only route left open is by appeal to human interiority: which is the converse of externality in public narrative space.

Modernists find the origins of religion in a sense of need for the divine which wells up from the subconscious into sensibility, where it takes the form of religious feeling or sentiment (not that this description would begin to do justice to the profound explanation of the 'exigence for the supernatural' in Blondel[6]). In a key sentence of the letter, *Pascendi* goes on:

> [T]his sentiment possesses, implied within itself both as its own object and as its intrinsic cause, the

reality of the divine, and in a way [it] unites man with God.[7]

The Modernist as theologian

Modernism is not, then, merely a humanism, nor does it deny divine agency in the world. But it confines this agency to subliminal impact on human interiority, an impact best described as 'sentiment'. Such divinely originated sentiment is not only the foundation and essence of the act of faith (that would merely be fideism, an attitude well known from earlier centuries). For the Modernists such sentiment is itself revelation as well. In different respects, it is both the subjective act of faith and the objective content of faith. Religious feeling is God's real though indistinct self-manifestation. Religious consciousness *is* revelation from which Modernists draw the conclusion that every religion is both human and divine – natural and supernatural – at the same time. To be sure, we must seek to distinguish between religions, and, come to that, degrees of adequacy of the expression of the same religion. But the criterion for doing will be the degree of development of religious consciousness implied. As Pius remarks, to Modernists the Catholic religion is no exception in this regard. As he writes:

> It is quite on a level with the rest; for it was engendered, by the process of *vital immanence*, in the consciousness of Christ, who was a man of the choicest nature, whose like has never been, nor ever will be ...

This is perhaps an attempt to capture the background

presuppositions of the French Modernist New Testament exegete Alfred Loisy.[8]

How, then, will a Modernist approach Scripture and Catholic dogma, with their accounts of revelation in Jesus Christ, involving such concepts as (for Scripture) Jesus Christ the Word and Wisdom of God, the Son of Man, the Only-begotten Son of God, and hence (for Catholic dogma) Incarnation and Trinity, and more specifically the hypostatic union of two natures, with their respective wills, in the single person of the God-man? The characteristic Modernist reply is as follows: the mind ponders the sentiment revelation generates, and produces initially spontaneous statements of a naive first order kind (compare Scripture), and then subsequently, more elaborated second order statements (compare dogma) which typically draw on the modes of thought of a given age. Neither the first order nor the second order statements can be said to possess absolute truth, in the way that the theses of scriptural inspiration and inerrancy, on the one hand, dogmatic infallibility on the other, would have it. Rather, the first, the Scriptural statements, are *symbols* of the revelation expressed in sensibility, the second, the dogmatic definitions, are *instruments* of it. Both, but especially the second, are to be judged by the extent to which they conduce to vitality of religious feeling. A doctrinal or theological formula, in order to be true, has only to correspond to the religious sentiment of the believer.

For the Modernist as doctrine-man, the key principles are, accordingly, symbolism and immanence.

First, then, there is the *principle of symbolism*. Since doctrinal formulae only symbolise their object, the sensibility which is God's indistinct self-revelation in human consciousness, they should be used when they are found helpful and otherwise discarded. As Pius puts it, Modernists would:

> have the believer avail himself of the formulas only in as far as they are useful to him, for they are given to be a help and not a hindrance; with proper regard, however, for the social respect due to formulas which the public magisterium has deemed suitable for expressing the common consciousness until such time as the same magisterium provide otherwise.

Secondly, still on the principles of the Modernist *qua* theologian, there is also the *principle of immanence*. Pius admits that an appeal to immanence can have an acceptable sense. Semi-quoting Augustine, it can be a way of saying God works in a way even more intimately present to me than I am to myself. But Modernists mean more than this. They mean that divine action always invests itself *in* the activity of nature: so revelatory divine action doesn't differ in principle from any other manner in which creative processes have divine causality behind them. The implication, thinks the pope, is pantheism – presumably of the kind associated with the seventeenth-century Jewish philosopher Baruch Spinoza where 'nature' and 'God' are treated indifferently as synonymous terms. Thus the Scriptures and the sacraments are expressions of a religious impulse based on the God who is within the human heart, as he is in all natural processes; and the Church herself simply represents the common consciousness of those whose religious vitality is shaped by the experiences of the first Christian believer, Jesus himself. And as that consciousness changes under the impact of new cultural epochs, so the meaning of her doctrines changes likewise – in order for them to continue to act as instruments of the religious sentiments originally found in the New Testament writings.

The Modernist as historian and critic

Speaking of the New Testament, what then about the Modernist as historian? Starting from the presupposition that divine action in external history is impossible, or at any rate cannot be registered by us, Modernist exegesis distinguishes between the Christ of history and the Christ of faith. In the New Testament texts, the human reality of the persons and events concerned has been, in the pope's word, 'transfigured' by being raised above its proper historical conditions, which is as much as to say that from the historical critic's viewpoint that reality has been *dis*figured. According to his real history, Christ was 'not God and never did anything divine'; moreover, 'as man he did and said only what they [the Modernists], judging from the time in which he lived, can admit him to have said or done'.[9] It is only in 'internal' history, in the movement of faith consciousness, that Jesus speaks and acts divinely, above all in the Gospel according to Saint John. In the spring of

1907, as it happened, the Anglo-German auto-didact Baron Friedrich von Hügel put the finishing touches to an article on the Gospel of St John, stressing its symbolic and non-historical character. It had been maturing for a while, in preparation for the great 11th edition of *Encyclopaedia Britannica*, the most scholarly incarnation of that monument of convenient information.[10] 'From beginning to end', declares the pope, 'everything in it [i.e. Modernist exegesis] is *a priori* and *a priori* in a way that reeks of heresy'.[11] The sacred books, and Pius singles out the Pentateuch (the first five books of the Bible) and the Gospels, have simply grown up incrementally – in a word, evolved – in order to adapt some primitive text to meet perceived changes in the needs of faith.

The Modernist as apologist

The Modernist as apologist naturally takes his own principles – agnostic, immanentist, evolutionist – into major account. Here Pius gives in effect a summary of Loisy's defence of Catholicism over against the German Lutheran historian of doctrine Adolf von Harnack. Modernist apologetics consists in showing that the seed planted by Jesus in his proclamation of a new divine Kingdom on earth has remained permanently immanent in the bosom of the Church: immanent but not inactive, since, in Pius's words, it:

> has gone on slowly developing in the course of history, adapting itself successively to the different mediums through which it has passed, borrowing from them

by vital assimilation all the dogmatic, cultural, ecclesiastical forms that served its purpose . . .[12]

No matter that the Church's Scriptures contain egregious errors in science and history: they were not designed to convey science and history but religious and moral experience. No matter that her dogmas contain flagrant contradictions: they were not designed to convey philosophical truth but to act as symbols for the Infinite. And Pius adds a coda: Modernists also employ an apologetic which some Catholics who reject immanence as a doctrine have imprudently made use of as well.

> They endeavour to persuade the non-believer that down in the very deeps of his nature and his life lie the need and the desire for religion, and this not a religion of any kind, but the specific religion known as Catholicism, which, they say, is absolutely postulated by the perfect development of life.[13]

What's wrong with that? The objection is that, in the manner in which they present this apologetic, they

> seem to admit that there is in human nature a true and rigorous necessity with regard to the supernatural order – and not merely a capacity and a suitability for the supernatural, such as has at all times been emphasized by Catholic apologists.[14]

Clearly, Blondel is in view here.[15]

The Modernist as Church reformer

Lastly, there is the Modernist as Church reformer.

Largely, what is at stake here is the reform of Church education: first and foremost, the abandonment of Scholasticism; the reconstruction of rational theology on the foundation of modern philosophy as represented by Modernism; the basing of positive theology on the history of dogma understood in the Modernist perspective.

Furthermore, Church authority must re-model itself on principles of governance found in the modern civil order, and, in accordance with the spirit of the contemporary world, the active virtues be stressed above the passive – meaning, presumably the contemplative.

'Pascendi': Conclusion and remedy

All in all, so Pius concludes, Modernism means the 'destruction . . . of the Catholic religion', and indeed of 'all' religion, inasmuch as the disproportion Modernists posit between human intelligence on the one hand, and the unknowable divine reality on the other, sets up an ultimately unsustainable tension. Modernism, so Pius predicts, will finish in atheism.

The remedy Pius proposes is closely allied to his analysis of the causes of Modernism. Modernism is 'born of the alliance between faith and false philosophy'.[16] Modernists recognise, says the pope, that the three chief difficulties for them are first, Scholastic philosophy, secondly the authority of the Fathers and Tradition more generally, and thirdly the magisterium of the Church, and on these they 'wage unrelenting war'.[17]

So Pius's first remedy is to renew the call of his predecessor Leo XIII for the use of Thomist philosophy in seminaries and religious study-houses. 'Let professors remember that they cannot set St Thomas aside, especially in metaphysical questions, without grave detriment'.[18] Dogmatic theology should then be built on this foundation, incorporating positive theology from the Fathers and the ecclesial magisterium, but not in such a way as to replace systematics by historical theology.

To the end that Modernist thinking be eliminated from the Church, the pope concludes by setting out a formidable programme of legal constraints: voiding for the future any theological doctorates awarded to those who have failed to study Scholastic philosophy; encouraging bishops to use the 'utmost severity' in granting permissions for the publication of theological works, and setting up diocesan 'watch committees' charged with 'noting the existence of errors and the devices by which new ones are introduced and propagated'.[19] Neo-Scholasticism from the pontificate of Pius X onwards, being framed as it generally was in terms of a response to Modernism, inevitably became associated with the mechanisms of doctrinal control put in place by the encyclical. This goes a long way towards explaining the *damnatio memoriae* it subsequently suffered, and the presumption that, if a more generous theological attitude were, with the Second Vatican Council, deemed desirable, the theological culture of the Church would have to turn its back on the inheritance of the immediate past.

Why 'Lamentabili' is here omitted

It seems to me that an analysis of *Pascendi* of the kind I have just offered suffices as an exposition of what Pius X understood by Modernism. I therefore consider myself excused from any obligation to fulfil the same office for what is often treated as its companion document, *Lamentabili sane exitu*, and for this omission I can give four supplementary reasons. First, as a decree of the Holy Office, simply, it lacks the authority of Pius's encyclical. Secondly, to understand its 65 condemned propositions in the sense in which they were found defective an adequate survey would have to take into account their contexts in the writings of contemporary Modernists: a task which, so far as I am aware, no one, surprising as it seems, has yet performed. Thirdly, to show in any coherent way the inter-connexion of these propositions would involve a substantial effort of doctrinal criticism which in the end would look remarkably like the text of *Pascendi*. Fourthly, as *Lamentabili* (promulgated on 3 July) precedes *Pascendi* (promulgated on 8 September) we can reasonably assume that anything substantial St Pius wanted to say or to have said on this subject should be sought in the later document more than the earlier.

Neo-Modernism: does it exist?

So without further ado I turn in the second part of this essay to the topic which represents its more *piquant* if also impressionistic element, and this is, in what sense or senses can we regard Modernism as *redivivus* in the second half of the twentieth century, the period from which we have only just emerged and when the vast majority of Catholic clergy and laity received their formation? Is there such a thing as Neo-Modernism, and if so where is it to be found?

To read traditionalist literature – which up to a point is a good thing to do, since in an age when Church life has been invaded by bureaucratic new-speak and pastoral emollience it is sometimes the only place to find a spade called a spade – one might get the impression that the entire intellectual life of the post-Conciliar Catholic Church has been an expression of Neo-Modernism from beginning to end. That is why I say it is a good thing to read traditionalist literature *up to a point*. The breaking point comes when the literature in question – as not infrequently – starts to flail about misdirecting its punches and indulging generally in wild rant.

In what sense, then, can we speak of a revival of Modernism in the last fifty or so years, and especially in the wake of the Second Vatican Council? A favoured term of Scholastic debate is *distinguo*, 'I distinguish'; and I would in fact like to distinguish here various senses in which that question might be understood. At least four come to mind.

Comprehensive Neo-Modernism

The first sense is, Neo-Modernism understood as a comprehensive revival of what I called earlier 'the Modernist *Weltanschauung*' – comprehensive because embracing all, or virtually all, the aspects which Pius X ascribed to that view of things. I think it would be difficult, though not impossible, to find the occasional post-Conciliar author for whom this would be the case. To reproduce historic Modernism in all its main aspects, albeit with some additional late twentieth-century spin is quite an achievement, may I say, given that the papal portrait of historic Modernism is what I called an 'identikit picture'. My most plausible candidate for this accolade would be the German priest-theologian cum psychologist Eugen Drewermann, a tardy disciple of Carl Gustav Jung, and the reason for saying so would be the key theme of his writing, namely, that we encounter divine revelation in the depths of the psyche, where it functions as a transformation of psychic archetypes.[20] If dogma or Church discipline fail to correspond with the felt experience of revelation, registered in shifting human sensibility, then so much the worse for them. At Drewermann's hands, exegesis, metaphysics, Christian doctrine, Church life – in fact all the interlocking dimensions with which *Pascendi* deals – have to 'morph' in order to meet this new paradigm which alone, Drewermann holds, does justice to human reality.[21]

Kernel Neo-Modernism

A second way to take the question, Where if anywhere is Neo-Modernism to be found, would be to ask after the common factor in the multiple dimensions identified in *Pascendi* and ask where if anywhere that common factor is alive and kicking. That common factor could be represented, it seems to me, by saying that where the objective patrimony of Catholic tradition appears no longer to suit human needs, then it is the patrimony which must be jettisoned – despite its claim to embody Tradition in the theological sense, that is, the transmission of divine revelation. If that is the heart of the Modernist attitude then I'm afraid I would have to agree that over the last forty years in particular a Neo-Modernist mind-set, in this limited but crucial sense, has been extremely common in the Catholic Church of the West. It is, I find, no pleasure to accumulate such references. One relatively authoritative example happens to be at my fingertips, and it comes from a publication of the French episcopate's pastoral centre for sacramental ministry, the *Centre des pastorales des sacrements*. In a 1975 document emanating from that Centre we read a statement that at any rate has the virtue of conciseness:

> When there is conflict between persons and the faith, it is the faith that has to bend.[22]

More widely, the reformation – better, deformation – of catechetics in the same period has been woefully affected by a negligence of, not to say hostility to, doctrine, on the grounds that the aim of catechesis is to disengage the implicit experience of grace already found in the depths of infant or adolescent or adult life – an experience which takes precedence over the doctrinal deposit entertained by the Church.[23] That attitude captures the *kernel* of Modernism even if it fails to find or chooses to ignore opportunities to follow through that basic option in all the subject areas to which Modernist thinking and sensibility could, if one wished, be applied.

So far, then, we have collected two senses in which we can, without massive exaggeration, detect Modernism revived: *either* a replication of the comprehensive Modernist attitude with its consequences for a variety of theological specialisms as well as Church life at large, *or* a reproduction of the kernel of the Modernist attitude, but shorn of its full range of reflective applications.

Sectorial Neo-Modernism

A third sense in which we can locate Neo-Modernism in the Church today can be called sectorial. It may be that a writer or school of writers have bought into Modernism in some particular aspect without necessarily either extending that to all areas described in *Pascendi* – comprehensive Neo-Modernism – or for that matter accepting as a key to Christian reality the subordination of the transmitted revelation to contemporary experience which I am going to call 'kernel Neo-Modernism'.

The most obvious manifestation of sectorial Neo-Modernism can be found in biblical studies, especially the study of the Gospels. The American Catholic exegete Luke Timothy Johnson, a laicized Benedictine priest teaching at a Methodist University and not, therefore, likely to exemplify 'right wing trash', has recently been expending most of his authorial energies on seeking to persuade Catholic exegetes not to ape the methods and consequently conclusions of their Protestant or more likely secular colleagues in the academy but to adopt a form of study of the Gospels more in keeping with the mind of the Church.[24] Centrally that means for him not contrasting the Jesus of history with the Christ of faith but to treat as our best historical guide to how it really was, *wie es eigentlich geschehen ist*, the portrait of Jesus as the God-man bringing salvation through his life, death and resurrection, mediated in a Spirit-filled Church, which is the overall upshot of the New Testament witness as a whole.[25] Much Catholic exegesis has become Modernist, in the sense in which the author of *Pascendi* would use that word in this area, even when the exegetes themselves in other respects may fully share the faith of the Church. Apart from any other considerations it can't be intellectually healthy to be so schizophrenic on the subject as to treat Jesus as a wandering charismatic from Monday to Friday (when in one's University department), and the uncreated Light from Light of the Nicene Creed on a Sunday morning (when in church). But that is an example of what I shall call sectorial as distinct from comprehensive or kernel Neo-Modernism.

Negative Neo-Modernism

My fourth and final sense of Modernism *redivivus* I shall call 'negative Neo-Modernism', and by that I mean theologies, philosophies, and spiritualities which signal departure from the mind of the Church by egregiously failing to meet the list of desiderata given by Pius X at the close of his encyclical. You may recall that the pope proposed three criteria for authentic catholicity if one wishes to be sure that, unwittingly or otherwise, one is not slithering into the mess of Modernist pottage described in the bulk of the letter. And they were: an ontology indebted to St Thomas; an expressive register privileging the texts of the Church Fathers and the other monuments of Tradition commonly accepted by the Church's approved divines; and a docility to the doctrinal leadership furnished by the magisterium.

Each of these three criteria merits a very brief comment. First, on the recommended philosophical wisdom: the ontology – the understanding of basic reality – of St Thomas, because it is a creation metaphysic which opens the way to a doctrine of God and the creature, is admirably suited to the further affirmations of the Creed, and represents in that regard a distillation of the wisdom of Christian antiquity in a perennial valid – which is not to say unimprovable – form. Ontologies highly different from his generally turn out to have major disadvantages for articulating Catholic truth.

Secondly, on the Fathers and Tradition: the Fathers, considered in their overall witness – the 'consensus' of the Fathers – provide the organ of reception in the Church of the biblical revelation. The Fathers register aright the content of that revelation, in its principal aspects and overall proportion. The other monuments of Tradition bear this out, as for instance the historic Liturgies of East and West, the primitive Creeds, iconography and so forth.

And thirdly and lastly, on the magisterium: just as without Tradition, including crucially the patristic witness, the Church would be disabled in her reception of Scripture, so without the magisterium she is disabled in her interpretation of Tradition. Scripture, Tradition and magisterium constitute for Catholicism an unbreakable circle, and distinctively Catholic theology recognizes this and makes sure it always moves in their ambit. One can see why on Pius's death in August 1914 Hilaire Belloc could write in *The British Review*:

> The note of Pius X's reign was simplicity. It stood composed of a few very clear principles like a carefully constructed classical thing of cut stone standing against a flood.[26]

What I am calling 'negative Neo-Modernism' (and I accept that the phrase is not a particularly perspicuous one) labels forms of thought in the Church that ignore Pius X's therapy for Modernism and in this way reproduce Modernism's lacunae, its gaps, though not its peculiar tenets, its positive if wrongheaded statements. Take the example of radical liberation theology. It would be difficult to think of a theology more at the antipodes from historic Modernism in what it positively asserts. Historic Modernism arises from a disproportionate emphasis on human interiority, on the importance of (especially) inner religious experience. Radical liberation theology, so far from reproducing this emphasis, abhors it, for it places divine agency not in the depths of the psyche but in the public square, in Kingdom-oriented socially transformative political activity. However, classical Christian ontology is as likely to be absent in such liberation theology as it is in Modernism, just as the Fathers are largely silenced in both, the other monuments of Tradition neglected in both, and the role of the magisterium marginalized in both. A great deal of contemporary Catholic theology commits these sins of omission of negative Neo-Modernism, typically lacking a strong metaphysical side, overleaping the Fathers and subsequent Tradition to join Bible and contemporary society in a would-be direct covenant, and leaving little place for papal and conciliar formulations. Among the post-Conciliar popes the teaching activity of John Paul II in particular could be described as governed by the imperative to neutralize negative Neo-Modernism by putting in place doctrinal instruments – such as the *Catechism* promulgated in 1992 – which emphasise a classical Christian ontology, the Fathers and other monuments of Tradition, and the teachings of Councils and previous popes.

A final paradox

I will leave readers with a paradox. On my definitions, Neo-Scholastic theology is itself to a degree guilty of negative Neo-Modernism. I say that on the ground of its poor record in including within its own corpus texts from the Fathers, references to the Liturgies, to iconography and to other instruments of Tradition. In that sense, the movements of patristic and liturgical *ressourcement* which fed into the so-called *Nouvelle Théologie* of the 1940s and 50s belong properly to Pius X's anti-Modernist reaction. Yet traditionalists remain suspicious of those movements as generating a theological culture that prepared the way for comprehensive Neo-Modernism, kernel Neo-Modernism, sectorial Neo-Modernism. Something has gone seriously wrong there with their judgment. But then something went wrong with the development of Catholic thought itself. It is the task of Catholics now to put it right.

Chapter Two

FOR NEO-GNOSTICS:
CHALLENGES TO ORTHODOXY
AND MISSION

A preamble

The vagaries of much contemporary theology would hardly have arisen without stimulus from the wider cultural environment in which the Church lives out her life. That environment furnishes opportunities, but it also contains snares. That is why Church authority must be crystal clear about criteria of discernment, so that the mind of the Fathers, which continues the mind-set of the apostles, may soak through Catholic consciousness in our own time also. The main aim of this second essay in *Criticising the Critics* is to present a document of the Roman magisterium which responds in the spirit of St Irenaeus to challenges from our contemporary religious situation, including what that second-century doctor – sometimes called the first systematic theologian of the Church – would surely have recognised as 'Neo-Gnosis'. That document is the 'Declaration' *Dominus Jesus*, published by the Congregation for the Doctrine of the Faith in the year 2000. The full title of *Dominus Jesus* is 'On the

Unicity [uniqueness] and Salvific Universality of Jesus Christ and the Church'. The hostile reception with which it met at the hands of theological liberals affected by Neo-Modernism may incline us to treat it with a certain *a priori* sympathy.

One might well link to *Dominus Jesus* a second, less familiar text, with which it has, however, a marked affinity. This is a document produced in 2003, under the title 'Jesus Christ, the Bearer of the Water of Life', by two other Roman entities, the Pontifical Council for Culture and the Pontifical Council for Interreligious Dialogue. This second document deals with the 'New Age'which, it may be said, bears a special resemblance to the Gnosis combated by Irenaeus. Like ancient Gnosticism, New Age is a contemporary invented religion of a more or less unorganised and certainly diffuse kind, rather than a long-standing religious tradition of thought and sensibility, with institutions of its own. While by its 'existence and fervour' New Age may constitute what these Curial writers call a 'witness to the unquenchable longing of the human spirit for transcendence and religious meaning',[27] its actual teachings, they say, function as an unacceptable surrogate for salvation in Christ, not least when the attempt is made to combine the two. New Age is, so these writers maintain, Gnosticism *redivivus*. Over against the (post-Christian) 'Age of Aquarius' announced by New Agers, the Roman authors proclaim the Word incarnate as the true Aquarius, the One who, at the well of Sychar, in converse with the Samaritan Woman (John 4: 1-15), showed himself the bearer of the water of life. (Hence of course the title of the second document to which, however, I shall make only occasional reference in what follows, so as to allow the first document its appropriate priority, as the work of the chief doctrinal organ of the Holy See.)

What we are seeing at Rome at the beginning of the new millennium is a tendency which could be called 'Neo-Irenaeanism'. In other words, there is a desire to unmask features of the contemporary scene that bear a resemblance to ancient Gnosticism, and to do so by rehearsing once again some of St Irenaeus's own major themes. A glance at the footnotes of *Dominus Jesus* and to the main text of *Jesus Christ, the Bearer of the Water of Life* will soon show the justice of this claim. It will, then, be appropriate to draw attention to a number of doctrinal similarities between *Dominus Jesus* and the thought of the second-century Church Father. The 1992 *Catechism of the Catholic Church*, which precedes the first of these documents by a short interval, carries, incidentally, no less than thirty references to Irenaeus: more than for any other Church father with the exception of Augustine. I may mention here one possible literary channel for this Neo-Irenaeanism: namely, the theological writings of the Swiss dogmatic theologian Hans Urs von Balthasar. Balthasar had a huge admiration for Irenaeus, whose writings he anthologised,[28] and on whom he wrote a dense monograph incorporated into volume II of his theological aesthetics.[29] His own systematic thought has been called by a recent American study a 'retrieval' of the theology of Irenaeus.[30] Furthermore, Balthasar considerably influenced the intellectual and spiritual outlook of both Pope John Paul II and, more especially, Cardinal Joseph Ratzinger, now Pope Benedict XVI, who expressed his debt to him in the funeral panegyric he preached for him at his burial in Lucerne on 1 July 1988. He was also the beloved mentor of the secretary of the Commission which produced the *Catechism*, the Dominican Archbishop of Vienna, Cardinal Christoph Schönborn.

The aims of 'Dominus Jesus'

The tone of *Dominus Jesus* indicates a certain background of anxiety. The desire to find common ground among the various world religions has led in some quarters to an attitude of religious indifferentism which no longer regards the work of Jesus Christ, in its biblical framework, as a revelation intended for the illumination and indeed salvation of the whole world: that is, a faith for all human beings without exception. But to limit the grace of Christ to one sector, merely, of divine saving operation, and thus deprive it of its globality, its comprehensiveness of aim, has to be judged an heretical opinion when we compare it with the witness of Scripture and of Tradition, as the latter is expressed in such 'monuments' as the Liturgy and the Fathers.

In addition to this principal preoccupation the Declaration *Dominus Jesus* also has a second, subsidiary but by no means unimportant concern. An analogous indifferentism, so it holds, besets inner-Christian ecumenism likewise. The desire to find common ground with other Christians has sometimes led liberal Catholics, in the period since the Second Vatican Council, to play down the claims to uniqueness of that Church body which is in peace and communion with the see of Peter, represented by the Bishop of Rome. Telling the truth about both kinds of issues – inter-religious dialogue and inner-Christian ecumenism – is pastorally desirable, because in both cases – though to different degrees – to suppress the demands of the Gospel mission and Catholic claims in the interests of pluralism and polite relations may also be to put others at a soteriological disadvantage. Not to know Jesus Christ and the blessings he brings the world is to be disadvantaged in relation to God. And similarly – or rather, analogously – not to know the full Gospel through the Church he founded in the integral transmission of these through time in a communion centred on the Roman bishop, Vicar of Peter, and thus Vicar of Christ, this is to be disadvantaged in relation to Jesus Christ and the blessings he brings the world. That at any rate is how orthodox Roman Catholics see it!

Dominus Jesus was not a wholly popular document in many quarters. Some liberal Catholics, who are disproportionally prominent in the media since they are more acceptable to secular elites, regretted it in its entirety. This was natural because the aim of later twentieth-century liberal Catholicism is to push against the limits of the documents of the Second Vatican Council in these matters, whereas the teaching office considers itself, on the contrary, to be bound by them. But the two halves of the document could also elicit contrasting reactions, often from the same people. Thus the first half pleased Evangelicals and the Eastern Orthodox. The second half did not.

The Introductory Chapter of 'Dominus Jesus': an Irenaean text

But it is time to see how the document unfolds. What the text is about is made plain in its introductory chapter. That introduction begins, as would any Protestant Evangelical, from the Great Missionary Command at the end of St Matthew's Gospel (Matthew 28: 18-20). The mission conferred on the Church by Jesus is universal, extending to all human beings, but the authors propose to concentrate more specifically on the implications of this mission for the existence of other religions. People already committed to other religions are not thereby withdrawn from the scope of the Church's mission. *Dominus Jesus* points out that, in calling for dialogue with representatives of the world religions, the Second Vatican Council by no means intended to substitute dialogue for mission. As the text has it: 'Such dialogue certainly does not replace, but rather accompanies the *missio ad gentes*'.[31] At this stage it could have been mentioned that the document of the Council on mission, which is a 'Decree', enjoys a higher magisterial status than the document on inter-religious dialogue which is only a 'Declaration', but perhaps that comparison was thought excessively technical. However, *Dominus Jesus* does not fail to footnote Pope John Paul II's

1991 encyclical on mission, *Redemptoris missio*, which makes exactly the same point about how dialogue is an internal accompaniment of mission, *not* an alternative to it.

For the Declaration *Nostra aetate* of the Second Vatican Council, such dialogue must be positive in character, willing to acknowledge whatever is 'true and holy in these [non-Christian] religions'.[32] Catholics are not Barthians, or even Calvinists. Moreover, not everything in the Church is fixed in stone: there are, even for orthodox Catholics, 'some fundamental questions [in this regard] that remain open to further development'. But 'theological reflections' worked out in the course of 'developing solutions' must always remain 'consistent with the contents of the faith . . .' as once given to the saints.[33] And that is precisely what has *not* invariably been happening. So what *has* been happening? The document observes:

> The Church's constant missionary proclamation is endangered today by relativistic theories which seek to justify religious pluralism, not only *de facto* but also *de jure (or in principle)*. As a consequence, it is held that certain truths have been superseded . . .

truths of which *Dominus Jesus* proceeds to list the chief examples. Here they are as stated in the Declaration:

[1] the definitive and complete character of the revelation of Jesus Christ,

[2] the nature of Christian faith as compared with that of belief in other religions,

[3] the inspired nature of the books of Sacred Scripture,

[4] the personal unity between the Eternal Word and Jesus of Nazareth,

[5] the unity of the economy of the Incarnate Word and the Holy Spirit,

[6] the unicity [i.e. the uniqueness] and salvific universality of the mystery of Jesus Christ,

[7] the inseparability – while recognizing the distinction – of the kingdom of God, the kingdom of Christ, and the Church . . .[34]

All these doctrinal headings are relevant, evidently, to the claims of the Gospel vis-à-vis the followers of other religions, and, as it happens, all of them in some form figured in Irenaeus's presentation of the faith 'against the heretics'.[35] That catalogue sums up many though not all the chief points Irenaeus himself would want to stress in any 'demonstration of the apostolic preaching'. (We can note in passing the absence of such Irenaean themes as the existence of only one God as Lord of creation, divine Providence through the Word, the congruence of the Old and New Testaments, the life of man as the vision of God.)

In this list of Irenaean motifs that *are* mentioned I have, so far, omitted to remark on one. And that is the danger, as the authors see it, of minimising the notable claims of the *Roman* Catholic Church in inner-Christian ecumenism. They express the truth they see at threat here in the words 'and the subsistence

of the one Church of Christ in the Catholic Church'
(as defined by communion with the Roman see). That
assertion is not without an Irenaean resonance, if we
bear in mind the emphasis of the celebrated primacy
text in *Adversus haereses* Book III, where the Bishop
of Lyons affirms that, if one wishes to know of the
contents of the *traditio apostolica* one can take a short
cut and look to:

> the most ancient church, the church known to all
> men, which was founded and set up at Rome by the
> two most glorious Apostles, Peter and Paul. For with
> this church, because of its position of leadership and
> authority, must needs agree every church, that is, the
> faithful everywhere; for in her the apostolic tradition
> has always been preserved by the faithful from all
> parts.[36]

(As the translation of this passage is sometimes
debated, I take the precaution of citing the English
version in a standard Anglican source.[37])

Such a catalogue of doctrines gives us in effect a
table of contents for the rest of *Dominus Jesus*. The
document, however, does not pass on to its exposition
of each endangered truth without first pausing to
suggest a source for the 'roots of these problems'
in what it calls 'certain presuppositions of both a
philosophical and theological nature, which hinder
the understanding and acceptance of the revealed
truth'.[38]

What 'presuppositions' do the authors have in
mind? They mean the kind of presuppositions which

fuel such questions as the following. [1] Is not divine truth essentially elusive, not to say inexpressible (=cognitive scepticism about revelation)? Is 'truth' not always the 'truth for me' – which might not be 'the truth for you' (=epistemological relativism)? Is not reason the only source of knowledge, so that no truth arising from an order that transcends reason can (or should) be acknowledged (=rationalism)? Again, how can there be truly ultimate – 'eschatological' – events which nonetheless show their presence in history (=empiricism)? And, finally, did the divine Word (the Logos) really become incarnate or is Jesus simply another religious phenomenon who symbolises that Word (=Christological reductionism)? The authors also blame two flaws in contemporary theological method: first, an eclecticism which is not bothered about 'consistency, systematic connection, or compatibility with Christian truth' and secondly, 'the tendency to read and to interpret Sacred Scripture outside the Tradition and Magisterium of the Church'.[39] Too often mired in these errors, doubts and methodological infelicities, contemporary Christians are left wondering, *Is* there a divinely revealed truth, given in history, whose content can be reliably known through Scripture and Tradition, a truth which sets out the basis for the salvation of all human beings? Rejecting the universal relevance of the 'rule of faith' found in the Church built on the apostles, the way is open to a New Gnosis.

Not all the philosophical and theological issues thus raised are pertinent to Irenaeus' situation but, uncannily, most of them are. Like Irenaeus, who was faced with radical heresies which had grown out of the Church by synthesising selected elements of New Testament Christianity with a syncretistic background sensibility, the Church today has to meet the challenge of distortions of the Gospel which appear more plausible because they chime more readily with a contemporary mind-set than does orthodoxy.[40] An egregious example of this is furnished by the heterogeneous movement called 'New Age'.

The uniqueness of salvation in Jesus Christ

The body of *Dominus Jesus* consists of six chapters and a conclusion. The three earlier chapters – on which I shall focus – are occupied with the issues raised by the existence of other religions – and these take up the bulk of the topics so far mentioned. The three later chapters, which stake out in very clear terms the claims of the Church of Rome, have for their subject the issues raised by inner-Christian ecumenism, and these concern in various ways the nature of the Church, though the closing chapter seeks to unify the document by linking ecclesiology to the soteriological aspect of a theology of world religions as laid out in Chapters I, II and III. I draw out what seem to me to be the most interesting or salient points made in the document's course.

Chapter I, entitled 'On the Fullness and Definitiveness of the Revelation of Jesus Christ', insists that any theory for which that revelation in Christ is 'limited, incomplete, or imperfect' and thus 'complementary' (merely) to that found in other religions, must be rejected as contrary to Christian faith.

> The truth about God is not abolished or reduced because it is spoken in human language; rather, it is unique, full, and complete, because he who speaks and acts is the Incarnate Son of God.[41]

As is well-known, it is a feature of Neo-Modernism to attempt to empty revelation of propositional content by insisting on its character as a personal relation set up between God and believers. Rather, says the document, faith involves a twofold adherence: to the God who reveals – personally then, as a living 'Thou', He Who Is, and yet also to the truth he reveals – precisely 'out of the trust which one has in him who speaks'.[42] This leads the authors to the drawing of an extremely important distinction. And that is the distinction between, on the one hand, faith in the properly theological sense of that word and, on the other, mere belief – as this is found in the non-biblical religions. Belief in this second sense is *not* the same as, or even a variant on, faith in the biblical-ecclesial understanding of that word: what Paul calls, on repeated occasions, 'the obedience of faith'.[43] *Pistis* is not *doxa*. Or to put it another way, divinely warranted belief is not human opinion. In the other religions, belief is, for *Dominus Jesus*, 'religious experience still in search of the absolute truth and still lacking assent to God who reveals himself'. Or in the text's fullest explanation of this difference:

If faith is the acceptance in grace of revealed truth, [the 'truth revealed by the One and Triune God'] ..., then belief, in the other religions, is that sum of experience and thought that constitutes the human treasury of wisdom and religious aspiration ...[44]

Clearly, that is an absolutely vital distinction for theological thought. The remainder of Chapter I is devoted to a corollary of this distinction. The sacred writings of other religions cannot be placed on the same level as the canonical Scriptures, whose human authors are hagiographs, men divinely inspired to produce the written record of the definitive revelation in history.

Chapter II of *Dominus Jesus* speaks of 'The Incarnate Logos and the Holy Spirit in the Work of Salvation'. For some writers, while the only economy of saving revelation God offers the world is indeed the economy of his eternal Word, that economy is not necessarily that of the *incarnate* Word. Wider than the limited economy of the Word incarnate, addressed to Christians, the eternal, invisible, uncreated Word has a more universal – broader, if less full – design for non-Christians, and this ampler plan does not require any reference to the Church. 'These theses', state the authors of *Dominus Jesus* in no uncertain terms, 'are in profound conflict with the Christian faith'.[45] The ecumenical Creeds rule them out in advance, though corroborative citations are also made from the Second Vatican Council and popes from Leo I to John Paul II. The key counter-assertion *Dominus Jesus* makes is this: since the Incarnation, 'all the salvific actions of the Word of God are always done in unity with the human nature that he has assumed for the salvation of all people'.[46] The mystery of Christ is co-extensive with all human history, since it extends from his election by God before time began right down to his glorious Parousia. Just read the opening chapter of the Letter to the Ephesians! Of course, the state of things *before* the Incarnation is somewhat different. If the divine Son, as Irenaeus could and does explain, mediates all knowledge of God, then as the pre-incarnate Word it was he who illuminated the minds of the Gentiles to find God in creation, and it was he who announced the Father to the patriarchs and prophets. But even then, so Irenaeus would insist, such visitations by the Word are all ordered to his Incarnation – to the definitive event of salvation that took place in Jesus Christ.[47] As the late Cardinal Jean Daniélou remarked:

> Irenaeus's characteristic, and original, contribution is his emphasis on the continuity between these earlier instances of the Word's presence among men and the Incarnation.[48]

Nor is the situation of theological dissenters any happier when, to posit an alternative economy to the one that passes through the incarnate Christ and his ecclesial community, they propose instead an independent economy of the Holy Spirit. The Spirit can never be separated from the Son. That is particularly Irenaean of course: one thinks of

Irenaeus's metaphor of the Son and Spirit as the 'two hands' of the Father.[49] The purpose of the economy of the Holy Spirit is precisely the actualization of the saving efficacy of the work of the Son, in relation to those who lived before Jesus and those who lived after him, as well as to his contemporaries. This is what Irenaeus calls in *Adversus haereses*:

> the Spirit preparing people in the Son of God, the Son leading them to the Father, and the Father giving them incorruptibility in eternal life which comes to everyone from the fact of seeing God.[50]

When the Holy Spirit sows 'seeds of the Word' (a famous phrase from Justin Martyr's *Second Apology*) in 'various customs and cultures', that is not in order to bypass Jesus Christ but rather so as to prepare them for 'full maturity in Christ': another citation in *Dominus Jesus* from the mission encyclical of John Paul II, *Redemptoris missio*.[51]

Chapter III, the last section of the document to deal with other religions, is entitled 'Unicity and Universality of the Salvific Mystery of Jesus Christ'. One might have thought that *Dominus Jesus* had by now made the assertion of this uniquely universal mystery quite unmistakably plain. What is left to be added? Before leaving the topic, the authors want to reiterate that the original apostolic preaching – preaching specifically of salvation through Jesus Christ – was made to a pagan world which 'aspired to salvation through a plurality of saviours'.[52] In this sense, there is no difference between the world of the apostle Paul, or of Irenaeus, and our own.[53]

At the same time, however, and here is if you will a 'liberal' element in the authors' thinking, they want to leave room for a theological exploration of whether and in what way the 'historical figures' and 'positive elements' of these religions – such figures as Gautama and Mohammed, such positive elements as Buddhism's call for asceticism towards temporal goods, Islam's call for submission to the one God – can be regarded as under certain aspects sub-mediations of the unique mediatorial being and action of Jesus Christ. What *Dominus Jesus* does here, tentatively – we note the words 'if [or 'whether'] and in what way' – is to transfer to the area of a theology of the world religions what Catholic doctrine has always maintained over against classical Protestantism in relation to the Mother of God and the saints. That is, there can be participations of Christ's unique mediatorship which do not overthrow the axiom stated in First Timothy 2:5, namely: 'There is one mediator between God and men, the man Christ Jesus'. If the only Mediator can enable sub-mediations of himself, then the rich power of his mediation is the more fully displayed. To the authors' minds, this does not necessarily compromise their claim that the saving work of Christ is unique, universal and absolute – and their rejection of the theological claim that the use of these terms in Catholic teaching is excessive, narrowing, and fundamentalistic.[54] It has not been much noted that this suggestion represents a remarkably audacious piece of innovatory theological thinking on the part of the Roman dicastery. We can compare with it what a North American patrologist has written of Irenaeus:

> Although he never specifically addressed the question, it is clear that Irenaeus would not conceive of revelations found in non-Christian religions as *alternative* means of knowing God *apart* from revelation through the Son. Whatever knowledge of God might be had by means of Hinduism or Buddhism would have to be mediated by Christ and be the result of the Father's will to make himself known to them for salvation.[55]

The uniqueness of the Church

Perhaps conscious of the temerity of their proposal, the authors of *Dominus Jesus* now return to safer ground, by rehearsing their reflections on the special status of *the Church*. In Chapter IV of *Dominus Jesus*, on the 'Unicity and Unity of the Church', the Congregation for the Doctrine of the Faith insists that, in their words:

> The Catholic faithful *are required to profess* that there is an historical continuity – rooted in the apostolic succession – between the Church founded by Christ and the Catholic Church.[56]

Here too *Dominus Jesus* can cite Irenaeus, side by side with two North African doctors, Cyprian and Augustine. To some – and that 'some' has included historically, most Lutherans – this emphasis on the apostolic succession may seem like a disproportionate concern with sacramental mechanics. But in fact it presents one important way of criticising New Age, not least as that movement is described by Paul Heelas in a study published by the Oxford University Press and cited approvingly in the pages of *Jesus Christ the Bearer of the Water of Life*. It is precisely the 'hierarchical organisation' of 'traditionalised religiosity', writes Heelas, that makes it 'well-suited for the community', whereas (he maintains) 'detraditionalised spirituality is well-suited [only] for the individual'.[57] That was also true of ancient Gnosis which, in the words of the American exegete Pheme Perkins, became a 'vehicle for internal migration rather than institutional external migration'.[58] But individuals *need* communities, not least so as to be fully *persons*.

But what exactly does *Dominus Jesus* mean by the phrase 'the Catholic Church'? This fourth chapter, by citing the Dogmatic Constitution of the Second Vatican Council *Lumen Gentium*, leaves its readers in little doubt. The Church of Christ, 'constituted and organised as a society in the present world', affirmed the conciliar fathers of Vatican II, 'subsists in the Catholic Church, governed by the Successor of Peter and by the bishops in communion with him'.[59] The exact force of that expression 'subsists in' – in the Latin, *subsistit in* – has been the subject of comment. The Congregation gives its own clarification when it writes:

With the expression *subsistit in* the Second Vatican Council sought to harmonize two doctrinal statements:

on the one hand, that the Church of Christ, despite the divisions which exist among Christians, continues to exist fully only in the Catholic Church, and on the other hand, that 'outside of her structure, many elements can be found of sanctification and truth', that is, in those churches and ecclesial communities which are not yet in full communion with the Catholic Church.[60]

In the upshot: Christian disunity is indubitably a 'wound' of the Church, hindering the attainment of her full universality, but it does not actually deprive her of the unity confessed in the Creed (there is *one*, holy, catholic and apostolic Church). Here *Dominus Jesus* echoes *Mysterium Ecclesiae*, an earlier 'declaration' (from 1973) of the same Roman Congregation, under Pope Paul VI:

> The Christian faithful are . . . not permitted to imagine that the Church of Christ is nothing more than a collection – divided, yet in some way one – of Churches and ecclesial communities; nor are they free to hold that today the Church of Christ nowhere really exists, and must be considered only as a goal which all Churches and ecclesial communities must strive to reach.[61]

Chapter V, 'The Church: Kingdom of God and Kingdom of Christ', tackles the 'low' or minimalising ecclesiology which would *contrast* the Church with the Kingdom, rather than seeing her as the Kingdom's '*seed* and *beginning*'.[62] While a variety of theological elucidations of the term 'Kingdom' are legitimate, all must maintain that the Kingdom can no more be disassociated from the Church than it can from Christ. To consider the Church at best an ambiguous sign of the Kingdom – a position often motivated by reaction against a 'presumed "ecclesiocentrism" of the past' – is 'contrary to Catholic faith'.[63] For Irenaeus too, the Church was

> the "glorious body of Christ" indwelt by the Spirit, whose operations in the world were co-extensive with the Church. It was the body in which Christ continued to fulfil the prophecies of the Old Testament ... In the whole world, as Irenaeus saw it, there was therefore no other way of ascent to God than through the Church.[64]

Rounding off the text

The sixth and final chapter rounds off *Dominus Jesus* by looking at 'The Church and the other religions in relation to salvation', in this way bringing the secondary, ecclesiological concern of the document into unity with its primary interest in how to evaluate other religions theologically. By his explicit assertion of the necessity of faith and Baptism for salvation the Saviour implicitly declared the necessity of the Church for salvation likewise, since these treasures are held within her house. That does not compromise God's universal saving will, since:

> [U]nited always in a mysterious way to the Saviour Jesus Christ her Head, and subordinated to him, [the Church] has, in God's plan, an indispensable relationship with the salvation of every human being.[65]

The Church, then, cannot be considered merely '*one* way of salvation alongside those constituted by the other religions' – and *a fortiori* (we may suppose) not alongside whatever hope of salvation might be associated with that *pot-pourri* of elements from the religions and elsewhere that is New Age. Rather, citing John Paul II's letter *Redemptoris missio*, the grace of Christ can give those outside the company of the baptized a 'mysterious relationship to the Church', which, while not formally incorporating them in her membership, nevertheless gives them a share in the 'enlightenment' which baptismal faith brings to her sons and daughters.[66] Here for a last time the name we find in the footnotes is, alongside Cyprian's, that of Irenaeus.[67]

Conclusion

Clearly, the See of Rome in the last years of John Paul II's pontificate saw Irenaeus as a privileged interlocutor for the doctrinal evils of our epoch. On the one hand, we can agree with the Anglo-Catholic Lionel Thornton in seeing in Irenaeus an outstanding witness to the faith of the ancient Church. In his *Revelation and the Modern World* Thornton wrote:

> As an exponent of Catholic orthodoxy St Irenaeus stands out as the most representative teacher of his time. . . . He is our most reliable guide to the structure of orthodoxy as it appears just after the last personal contacts with the apostolic age have been finally severed. In this way he is the authoritative exponent

of a tradition which is coterminous with the New Testament and which overlaps it.[68]

But more than this, the modern Romans are saying, owing to the return of a number of the errors his theological doctrine corrects and the simultaneous emergence of a New Gnosis, he is a Father and doctor tailor-made for our own time.

Chapter Three

FOR ACADEMIC EXEGETES: READING SCRIPTURE IN THE CHURCH

Introduction

I sometimes ask clergy, How much did you get out of biblical studies in your Ordination training at theological college, seminary, university, ministerial training scheme, or whatever? How much did you take away that has been genuinely useful to you since? I did a diploma at Oxford which occupied at least half of my time for six terms, and I have to say that very little of it has been of any help to me subsequently, whether as a priest or a religious, whether for reciting the divine Office, taking part in the liturgy of the Word, or for preaching, instruction of converts, or even for writing theology. Far too much time was spent on questions of authorship, provenance, the tracing of sources for biblical books, the Synoptic problem, the issue of who influenced whom, and questions that, in retrospect, seem more like thesis topics for doctoral students looking around for a subject, such as who were St Paul's opponents at Corinth, or what is the relation of St John's Gospel to early Gnosticism. Having spoiled a perfectly good copy of the Jerusalem Bible by, as instructed, marking the Pentateuch in four colours for J, E, D, and P, it was especially annoying to find, twenty five years later, that the Wellhausen hypothesis no longer reflects a scholarly consensus – not that, in reality, it ever did, but the sort of works that showed it didn't never got on to my reading list.

Both my Oxford tutors were Anglican clerics, and all my lecturers were Anglicans save one who was a Congregationalist. Not that it is very likely, in the English context, that matters would have been different had they been Catholics. In Anglo-Saxon countries, at least, the study of Scripture by the historical-critical method, whether in universities or by university-trained teachers in Church institutions, had by the 1970s very largely ceased to be a confessionally determined or even confessionally influenced affair. It was, in the words of the French Dominican scholar François Dreyfus, *exégèse en Sorbonne*, Scripture in the academy, rather than *exégèse en Eglise*, Scripture in the Church.[69] Except – and this was the paradox – it was in practice Scripture in the academy transferred to the Church and, in any case, by the later twentieth century the academy would be unlikely to take any interest in Scripture were it not for the continued existence of the Church. Here and there, of course, an alternative approach could be found – among conservative Evangelicals, conservative Roman Catholics, the Orthodox. But so far as the exegetical culture of the great study centres was concerned, and the books reviewed and the articles written in the principal academic journals, these were almost completely off the radar screen.

Dreyfus who, as his name suggests, was Jewish by background, and perhaps that difference helped him, was among the first, in the mid 1970s, to mount a rearguard action. His master-idea, laid out in the pages of the *Revue Biblique*, the journal of the *Ecole biblique et archéologique française de Jérusalem*, was a comparatively simple one. The 're-actualisation' of texts, by which he meant their *re-invigoration in new contexts as a divine plan works itself out in history* – a process which, as historical critics themselves bore witness, explains the formation of the biblical corpus – could only be continued, in the case of the New Testament, in the community which formulated the biblical Canon and lived with the Scriptures in liturgy and preaching. That is, of course, the community of the Church. Dreyfus' voice was, in the 1970s, distinctly isolated (one might even call it, in some words from the Stanbrook Abbey hymnal, 'derided and denied'). Today, however, at the end of the 2000s, it sounds much more like a herald of the future (though, come to think of it, St John the Baptist, to whom the Stanbrook Office hymn was dedicated, was himself exactly that).[70]

A Cistercian from Hungary (via America)

But now let us look at a few more recent straws in the wind. The Cistercian Denis Fárkasfalvy, a member of the Pontifical Biblical Commission and abbot of the monastery of Our Lady of Dallas at Irving, Texas, has worked on the interface between the New Testament and the apostolic Fathers. He has also, significantly, produced a study of the exegesis of St Bernard of Clairvaux. In a 1998 article entitled 'A Heritage in Search of Heirs: the Future of Ancient Christian Exegesis', Fárkasfalvy deplored the fact that biblical studies today have 'amazingly little to say about the fundamental concepts on which ancient exegesis is based'.[71]

> We mention here only the most important topics: the unity of the two Testaments, the oneness of a universal salvation history centred on Christ, the uniquely privileged role of the biblical word in the process of God's self-disclosure, and the law of incarnation pervading the process from Adam through Abraham to Christ.[72]

To these he added, and underlined the addition, the doctrine of prophets and apostles as ministers of the covenants and accredited ministers of the divine Word in the context of a community of salvation. In Fárkasfalvy's judgment, contemporary scholars have come to treat the notion of, in particular, apostolicity as no better than ecclesiastical propaganda – an attempt at the manipulation of texts by those seeking to forward a theological agenda. Fárkasfalvy considered this an especially serious case of the general syndrome, since, when the validity of the idea of apostolicity is called into question, its foundational role for the Canon of Scripture is undermined.

In effect, then, the Bible has been cut off from its

ancient – and, of course, its mediaeval – interpreters. As currently dissected by mainstream historical-critical exegetes, the Scriptures are increasingly in danger of fading into 'existential irrelevance'.[73] This is so not least because

> the whole system of the critical and historical method, imposed very rigidly on the biblical text and possibly in a more relaxed way on the patristic sources, remains under the tyranny of historical rationalism, demanding that, in the name of scholarly objectivity, all doubt about "what really happened"... be kept on the highest possible level of alert, while all references to the transcendental or supernatural be programmatically left out and the discourse be reduced to the critical level.[74]

And Fárkasfalvy concluded:

> Like Pilate in the gospel narrative we have posted guards over the tomb of Jesus . . . and thus assure [sic] that nobody would legitimately speak of his Resurrection, while, in fact, the creation of all patristic and mediaeval exegesis – one must also include the very composition of the gospels – took place in the light of the Resurrection as the one constitutive event of Christian faith. It is no wonder that, ultimately, a wide abyss remains between us and the exegetes of the ancient Church.[75]

A Jesuit from Belgium (via Rome)

Ignace de la Potterie, whose main work was a three volume study in French of the idea of truth in the

Johannine writings, is a Belgian Jesuit who taught at the Biblicum, the Pontifical Biblical Institute in Rome, until his death in 2003. In an essay of 1986 – chronologically half-way between Dreyfus' manifesto and Fárkasfalvy's American offering – de la Potterie had asked, 'Is the patristic way of reading the Bible still possible today?' In 'Reading Holy Scripture "in the Spirit"', de la Potterie didn't scruple to call much critical exegesis 'methodologically atheistic'.[76] He argued that the overall orientation of thought and culture in the countries of the Continental Reformation, Germany above all, where scientific exegesis had its cradle, was deeply affected by the rationalism first made philosophically fashionable by the Dutch-born thinker Baruch Spinoza. Rationalism as embodied in Spinoza requires the resolution of every problem by the resources of reason alone. Fárkasfalvy claims that contemporary academic biblical scholarship has fallen under the tyranny of historical rationalism. De la Potterie provided a genealogy for this collapse. It was under the influence of Spinoza's rationalism that textual exegesis was required to 'deny itself any other dimension, ignore all opening to transcendence, exclude the meddling of faith'.[77] This exclusivist rationalism triumphed fully in the eighteenth-century Enlightenment which explicitly rejected tradition as a means of accessing truth and confirmed reason's total autonomy. The nineteenth century proceeded to add the contribution of historicism, the affirmation that reality is history and nothing but history. Thus by the start of the twentieth century the ambience in which the scholarly study of Scripture was carried on could be cumulatively described as 'historicist positivism'. On de la Potterie's analysis, this is the new form of the immanentism initiated by Spinoza.

> The illusion of historicism was to believe that, by the rigorous application of historical criticism, that is, in cutting off the higher layers of the Gospels (which were added by faith, as they said, and so to be considered as "mythical"), one could at last extract authentic Christianity, that of the "historical Jesus".[78]

Making his own some words from the Rumanian cultural anthropologist Mircea Eliade, de la Potterie commented astringently that such historicism is in reality not a rediscovery of Christianity but a product of its 'de-composition'. '[I]t could only have come about insofar as we had lost faith in the trans-historical reality of the historical event.'[79] And he reminded his readers that *Dei Verbum*, the Dogmatic Constitution of the Second Vatican Council on Divine Revelation, had taught that God reveals himself *in* history by what the Constitution calls 'events and words intimately linked'.[80] Yet since that Council, a happy rediscovery of Scripture by an extension of the monastic practice of *lectio divina* in which many of the faithful seek to study the Bible in order to understand their Christian faith better and live it more personally, has failed to awaken any corresponding echo amongst exegetes themselves. Exegesis is still regarded 'principally if not exclusively as a philological and historical science'.[81] Speaking descriptively, not prescriptively:

[Exegesis's] role is to show where texts come from, what their genesis is, and what meaning they might have for their first readers. Thus one strives to reconstitute historical and literal *facts*.[82]

But, de la Potterie goes on to ask:

Is this sufficiently attentive to the *meaning* of texts, to *their whole meaning*? Shouldn't we recognize that some sort of belief is required even in their search for "meaning"?[83]

De la Potterie's strategy is to draw in the philosophers: more specifically, two German philosophers of the twentieth century. First, he brings to the witness-stand Martin Heidegger who argued that interpretation is really explication – *Aus-legung*, a 'reading-out' of the meaning of a text by disengaging whatever is implicit in its contents, and in that way bringing to light its hidden riches. De la Potterie finds that strictly analogous to the effort of the Fathers to discover beneath the letter Scripture's spiritual sense. His second witness is Heidegger's younger contemporary Hans-Georg Gadamer for whom it is, precisely, a *tradition* that renders explicit the latent virtualities of texts. Gadamer

denounced the naiveté of historicism, which wants to be able to treat the historical given as an object [whereas] . . . the authentic understanding of a human phenomenon requires that one keep in mind its effectual history (*Wirkungsgeschichte*). To interpret is . . . to go . . . beyond words, in order to reach the profound life that emerges progressively from the "effectual history".[84]

Interpretation, so understood, gives language life beyond the immediate where and when of its earliest utterance. With this philosophical conclusion de la Potterie compares a text from his beloved Johannine corpus: 'When the Spirit of truth comes, he will lead you to the complete truth'.[85] This the Paraclete does when later Christians read the Scriptures according to the same Spirit as that by which they were written.

For de la Potterie, the history of Catholic exegesis in the second half of the twentieth century is the story of a derailment. When the founder of the Jerusalem *Ecole biblique*, the Dominican Marie-Joseph Lagrange, threw his weight behind the study of Scripture by the historical-critical method or what Lagrange himself called investigating the 'humble grammatical sense',[86] this was, for him, a harsh necessity of the times, since otherwise at a time of intensive discussion of the biblical text by both Protestant and sceptical scholars the Catholic voice would simply not be heard. It was never, so de la Potterie insists, Lagrange's intention that Church exegesis should stop short at this level. Evidence supports de la Potterie's view. In a letter published by de la Potterie's Jesuit confrère Henri de Lubac, one of Lagrange's closest collaborators reported how 'Père Lagrange never tired of warning his hearers against what he unhesitatingly called "the vain pretensions of historical exegesis".'[87]

How many times in frequent scriptural discussions during our long years of labour together, did I hear him deplore the fact that the harsh demands of the task which was dictated by the needs of the period restricted us to the intricate area of historical exegesis and deprived us of the opportunity of personally enjoying the rich fruits of spiritual exegesis, whose different points of view will never exhaust the treasures of meaning enclosed by God in the Scriptures whose author he is.[88]

And writing to de Lubac himself, the same correspondent, Hugues Vincent of the *Ecole* stressed that

even though the needs of the moment required [Lagrange] to devote the major part of his work to basic literal and historical exegesis, he still considered a spiritual interpretation of the Word of God, based on the powerful and profound spirit of the Fathers of the Church . . . to be no less indispensable and much more fruitful for the soul.[89]

A good example of what Lagrange had in mind is furnished, I think, by de Lubac himself when he wrote in his very influential book *Catholicisme*, originally published in 1938:

The whole of the Old Testament is habitually seen by the Fathers as one comprehensive and extensive prophecy, and the subject of the prophecy is no less than the mystery of Christ which would not be complete were it not also the mystery of the Church.[90]

A Bavarian pope

In the year 2000, Ignace de la Potterie put together

a book of reprinted essays, including one by de Lubac, on 'Christian exegesis today'.[91] This venture would hardly have caused much stir in the French-speaking world had not one of the contributors been Cardinal Joseph Ratzinger, not long after to become pope as Benedict XVI. As is well-known, the Pope has since spent much of his spare time writing a two volume book on the Founder of Christianity, the first volume of which, containing in its opening chapter a discussion of method in biblical study, has already appeared. A perusal of that chapter makes it plain that the Pope does not propose to shut down – even if he could! – the Catholic study of the Bible by the historical-critical method. Indeed, he calls that method not only permissible but essential and therefore compulsory. Why so? Because, he says, it follows from our faith in the Incarnation of the Word which entails his historicity and therefore facticity, and thus grounds the legitimacy of seeking to approach him by means of historical research. But Benedict is equally adamant that the inherent limitations of the historical method need to be recognized. As currently practised, this method assumes the 'uniformity of the context in which the events of history unfold'.[92] It assumes that history is homogeneous, that events happened then as they do now and will in the future. And by assuming likewise that history constitutes a closed system it excludes definitionally any role for divine action and in this way renders the very concept of salvation history – not to put too fine a point on it – a contradiction in terms.

Knowing that some of his readers would themselves be professional exegetes, though, to be sure, his book is a work of what the French call *haute-vulgarisation*, Benedict seeks to shake a little their philosophical confidence. Experience teaches us, he points out, that human utterances express, or signify, more than what their speakers or writers intend. Why should that not apply to the Bible as well? Furthermore, the historical-critical method has itself uncovered in Scripture a dynamic of remembering and retelling, as well as anticipating and prophetically interpreting. It finds in the Bible a state of affairs where texts point beyond themselves – whether back into the past or forward into the future. (Here what the Pope says reminds one of Dreyfus' audacious articles of the 1970s with their message of 're-actualisation'.) Who, then, does the historical critic think he or she is in staking a claim to decide, on behalf of these texts, what it is that ultimately moves the process of history? Dreyfus would say, the critic 'in the Sorbonne' is not their accredited re-actualiser. Where the meaning of the biblical history is concerned, theirs is not the final word.

A British voice

This, so the English may say, is all fine and dandy, but it is a long way from home: Rome, Jerusalem, even the Lone Star State. I can report it has now arrived in Oxford having first sojourned in Cambridge. Dr Markus Bockmuehl, an Anglican of Swiss Reformed background but born in Canada, previously a lecturer at Cambridge and Fellow of Fitzwilliam and now Professor of New Testament Studies at Keble College, Oxford, has rallied to just the sort of approach the writers I've been describing represent. 'To read Scripture predominantly as a document of ancient religion', wrote Bockmuehl in his essay 'Reason, Wisdom, and the Implied Disciple of Scripture', to be found in a collection edited in 2003 by two Cambridge professors, David Ford and the late Graham Stanton, is an 'elementary category mistake' which confuses genesis with meaning,[93] a point already made, though Bockmuehl may well be unaware of the fact, by de la Potterie. Bockmuehl compares historical-critical exegetes who adopt a skeptical or even a neutral posture towards their subject-matter to 'restricting the study of a Stradavari to the alpine softwood industry of Trentino'.[94] The inevitability of reductionism in such an approach to Scripture is not only religiously unfortunate. It is intellectually indefensible. '[T]he historic significance of the ancient biblical texts is inseparable from the space they have inhabited, and continue to inhabit, as the canonical Scripture of the Christian Church.'[95] According to Bockmuehl, the negative consequences for theology are pretty disastrous, notably in Britain. The Babylonian captivity of the Bible in an academy hostile to Christian presuppositions has brought about a situation where present-day systematic theology in the United Kingdom betrays, to Bockmuehl's eyes, a 'studied avoidance of any formally articulated engagement with Scripture'.

> With painfully few exceptions, it fails to pay so much as lip-service to the idea that Christian theology derives in any palpable sense from Scripture.[96]

Even Archbishop Rowan Williams whom he partially exonerates from this charge scores only a beta in Bockmuehl's marking-scheme. Archbishop Williams' approach is vitiated by his antipathy towards what Bockmuehl calls 'integrated canonical readings' which, by seeking to show that the overall testimony of Scripture is in this or that respect a unified message, become vulnerable to dismissal as 'uncritical' or 'totalitarian'.

> To brand dissent from relentlessly conflict-driven readings as "fundamentalist" does little to redeem [the archbishop's] lack of a coherent sense of Scripture as in any sense the divine word of life.[97]

This is a harsh judgment but it is motivated by Bockmuehl's concern for what he calls the 'intended reader' of Scripture. This reader he identifies as 'the disciple', situated within the community that hears the Word, and engaging with the 'implied text' that is Scripture's witness to the Christ. Though the general tenor of Bockmuehl's essay might be described as Evangelical, he begins his section on the implied disciple by declaring:

> For the biblical and patristic writers, the interpretation of Scripture is itself subject to the hermeneutic of the Spirit: prophetic truth is never just a matter of *individual* interpretation.[98]

The ending of Bockmuehl's piece is especially striking. This deals with an episode attested in two early lives of St Thomas Aquinas. Wrestling with the meaning of a passage in the Book of Isaiah for three days of prayer and fasting, Thomas eventually found a resolution in a preternatural conversation with the apostles Peter and Paul. According to an inscription on an Antwerp engraving of 1610 which Bockmuehl uses to illustrate his essay, the twin apostles 'often used to teach him in difficult questions'. Without necessarily underwriting the claim to heavenly visitations (though saying nothing to distance himself therefrom), Bockmuehl describes Thomas as 'prompted and accompanied in this evidently communal and ecclesial task' of studying Scripture and working at it 'not in splendid isolation but as a disciple in the company of the saints'.[99] Correctly, Bockmuehl points out how it is only in recent years that the importance for Thomas of biblical exegesis has been recognized and Thomas's own excellence as a reader of the Bible appreciated at its full worth.

In the sermon which marked Thomas's inauguration as a master of theology, a text rediscovered at Florence in 1912, he commended Scripture for fulfilling St Augustine's three-fold mission to any speaker: to teach the ignorant, to delight the bored, to change the lazy.[100] Scripture does exactly these three things, says Thomas in the sermon. It 'firmly teaches with its eternal truth'. It 'sweetly delights with its pleasantness'. It 'efficaciously changes with its authority'.[101]

A word from a Synod

I would like to finish with a vignette from, in one sense, Rome again, but in another sense from the Latin and Oriental churches in communion with Rome, since my source is the 'Message to the People of God' of the Synod of Bishops on 'The Word of God in the Life and Mission of the Church' which ended its deliberations on 26 October 2008. The message, which can be downloaded from the Vatican website, is quadripartite: section 1 is on the 'voice of the Word': revelation; section 2 is on the 'face of the Word': Jesus Christ; section 3 is on the 'house of the Word': the Church; section 4 is on the 'roads of the Word': the mission of the Church. Perhaps I can decant for you a few droplets which go nicely with the content of this essay. The bishops speak of the Word of God as preceding and going beyond the Bible which itself, however, as 'inspired by God',[102] contains that same efficacious divine Word.

> Precisely because the capacity of the divine Word embraces the Scriptures and yet extends beyond them, the constant presence of the Holy Spirit who "will lead you to the complete truth" [one notes that is the same verse, John 16: 13, highlighted by de la Potterie] is necessary for those who read the Bible.[103]

They go on to identify this Spirit-led reading of the Bible with the *Paradosis*, the 'great tradition'.

> This is the great Tradition: the effective presence of the "Spirit of truth" in the Church, guardian of the

Sacred Scriptures, which are authentically interpreted by her magisterium.[104] This Tradition enables the Church to understand, interpret, communicate and bear witness to the Word of God.[105]

The Synod recognizes, however, that the Bible is letter as well as spirit. Scripture's 'fleshly' dimension calls for an historical and literary analysis. The Bible is expressed, as it admits, in 'particular languages, in literary and historical forms'.[106] But the 'Message to the People of God' goes on to emphasise that Scripture mediates nonetheless the 'eternal and divine Word', and for this reason requires additionally 'another kind of understanding, given by the Holy Spirit who unveils the transcendent dimension of the divine Word, present in human words'.[107] And so:

> Exegetical knowledge must therefore weave itself indissolubly with spiritual and theological tradition so that the divine and human unity of Jesus Christ and Scripture is not broken.[108]

The synod bishops underline the 'profound and intimate unity of Scripture'. In what I guess to be an echo of St Paul's 'one Lord, one faith, one Baptism', they stress how there is 'one Canon, one dialogue between God and humanity, one plan of salvation'.[109] The Bible has as its intended centre Christ himself (here they touch on one of Fárkasfalvy's forgotten themes) who 'retrospectively sheds his light on the entire development of salvation and history and reveals its coherence, meaning, and direction'.[110] It is because at the centre of revelation the divine Word has acquired a *face* that the ultimate goal of biblical knowledge is an 'encounter with an event' – indeed, 'with a person' – and of a kind that 'gives life a new horizon and a decisive direction': words borrowed from Benedict XVI's first encyclical, *Deus caritas est*.[111]

We may not always associate bishops with silence, despite St Ignatius of Antioch making silence the way the bishop iconises the Father. This 'Message' at any rate ends, rather movingly, in an appeal for silence:

> Let us now remain silent, and hear the Word of God with effectiveness, and let us maintain this silence after hearing, so that it may continue to dwell in us, to live in us, and to speak to us. Let it resonate in us at the beginning of our day so that God may have the first word and let it echo in us at the evening so that God may also have the last.[112]

Chapter Four

FOR FEMINISTS:
HOW GOD IS FATHER

Introduction

The hymnology of the Latin Church calls Jesus Christ, the Son, 'Father of the world to come'; and the Paraclete, the Holy Spirit, 'Father of the poor'. But it is the first Trinitarian person who is the paternal origin not only of the world made through Son and Spirit, but also of the Son and Spirit – fatherly though they be under certain aspects. Though feminists would also avoid these (rather rarely used) titles of the Son and Spirit, the real bugbear for theological feminism is the naming of the first divine person: the 'Father' *par excellence*.

I shall, then, devote the bulk of my exposition to a 'paterology', that is, to a theology of the first person of the Trinity (though this, as we shall see, is impossible without reference to Son and Spirit). On the way I shall treat three critical issues which have divided Christians, whether ancient or modern, in their thinking about this primordial *credendum* with which the historic Creeds of Christendom begin: 'I believe in God, the Father almighty'. Next I will suggest some ways in which the occlusion of the being and activity of the Father in creation, revelation and salvation has had a deleterious effect on the culture of the West. And in conclusion I will indicate how the objections, whether theological or cultural, that have been made to the orthodox Christian theology of the Source of the Trinity, the divine Father, can be removed if, as some of the finest twentieth-century Catholic theologians have proposed,[113] the specifically Christian doctrine of God is construed – certainly not exclusively and yet above all – in the light of the Cross.

The revelation of the Father

That God is our Father is the manifest claim of the New Testament, but to scan this claim successfully we need the interpretative assistance of Tradition to see what such words might mean. The influential liberal Protestant theologian and historian of doctrine Adolf von Harnack, for example, wanted to restrict the 'essence of Christianity' – *das Wesen des Christentums* – to acknowledgement of the unique value of everyone, conceived in the framework of belief in the fatherhood of God. Harnack's hostility to the Church's dogma made him miss the fact that the New Testament revelation of God as Father is neither simply nor even primarily the attribution of certain qualities to the divine nature. It is not only, or even mainly, a statement about the provident care and tender mercy of One who knows every sparrow that falls to the ground, and considers human beings of more worth than any sparrow – though, to be sure, the

Gospels include such affirmations. Yet those qualities of the truly caring parent who is ever-attentive to the welfare of their children had already been ascribed, in Israel's tradition, to the God of the patriarchs, who was also the God of Moses and of David, and so united in himself all the covenant relationships which bound the chosen people to their Lord through these human mediators. Indeed, in the canticle recited by the dying Moses in the book of Deuteronomy, YHWH is explicitly named as 'father' of his people, with an emphasis on both divine authority and divine longsufferingness.

> Do you thus requite the Lord, you foolish and senseless people? Is not he your father, who created you, who made you and established you?[114]

Of course, the New Testament confirms the Old, and nothing of the Judaic doctrine of God – his transcendence of, yet presence in, his creation, and notably his freely willed co-involvement with his chosen people – is alien to the teaching of Jesus and the faith of the apostolic Church. But the New Testament is far from *merely* confirming, in matters of the doctrine of God, its Old Testament inheritance.

What we must now take into account is the Paschal Mystery. Already hinted at in sayings of Jesus about his peculiar relation of intimacy to God, and the embodiment of the divine claim in him, as well as about the power of the Spirit at work in his words and actions, there took place at the first Easter a veritable explosion of divine glory. Or, to put that in terms less of biblical aesthetics, vital as its categories are for expressing the overwhelming wonder of what happened then, and more in terms of religious semantics: a company of Jews (and Jewesses) who, through their sharing the faith of Israel, possessed a true grasp of the divine reality, were suddenly confronted with a super-abundance of fresh meaning. As they saw things, in the combined events of his suffering, death and resurrection, Jesus, the ultimate prophet and definitive divine legate, did not simply vindicate the claims he had made about the divine nature and his place in the working out of the divine plan. More than this, there took place in those events a new disclosure of the divine that was, for the world, redemptive in force. To shift to the present tense which came so readily to their lips (or pens): in the bestowal on the risen Jesus of a real – tested and proven – lordship over nature and history, God reveals Jesus, the Crucified, to be the divine Son – and therefore, by the same token – reveals *himself* to be quintessentially the divine Father. And this God does by the illuminating power of the Holy Spirit now sent on the disciples from the Father through the Son as the Spirit brings the disciples of Jesus, restored and forgiven, into a share in the love-life of Father and Son by means of what the New Testament calls *huiosis*, adoption as sons (and daughters).

In the founding happening of the Christian tradition, we are dealing not simply with a redemptive action of a God who is, on the basis of the Old Testament, already known, but with a redemptive revelation which has as its issue the life-transforming impact on us of the supreme truth that the saving God is the Holy Trinity. As that catholicising Presbyterian, the Scots theologian Thomas Torrance, put it:

> In ourselves as contingent beings we are confined within the limited range of our creaturely consciousness and perception, but under the impact of God's self-revelation in Jesus Christ and the creative operation of his Holy Spirit our minds and capacities are opened and our thoughts are expanded far beyond their finite limits until they are made appropriate, in some measure at least, to their divine object.[115]

And in the first place what this means is the discovery that God is primordially the Father.

We are so used to thinking – in philosophical or quasi-philosophical contexts, in conversations with other monotheists such as heterodox Christians and Jews, and in explanations of ourselves to agnostics and secularists – that God is the Creator, we forget the fact that for the Creeds there is something even more primordially true. God is the *Father* far more fundamentally than he is the Creator, for he generated the only-begotten Son before all worlds. The victory of the Nicene party, with in the East St Athanasius and in the West St Hilary at their head, in their struggle for recognition as authentic witnesses to the deep mind of the Church, was the triumph of that orthodox Christology which alone makes full sense of the New Testament records. Since God himself was in Christ reconciling the world to himself, Jesus is not, in his ultimate personal identity, a creature as we are, for of no creature could it be said that its actions were those of God himself. But Athanasius's victory meant more still. The triumph of the Nicene Symbol vindicated faith in God as the essentially fruitful One – the Father: he whose loving generativity expressed in the eternal procession of the Uncreated Son gives us the key for understanding the basic relation of God to the world.

If the world is not a necessary work of God; if, as Scripture indeed presents it, it is not the unfolding of the divine being (this would be some form of pantheism) but a work as freely made as that of any artist, then we *might* be justified in thinking of creation as, so to speak, thrown off by God gratuitously, taking 'gratuitously' there to be synonymous with 'atypically' or even 'carelessly'. Perhaps, if the world be (as it is) God's free creation, God regards it as something of an experiment. Possibly he may see the experiment, at least so far as man is concerned, as rather a failure, on which the files will in due course be declared closed. But the Creed's authoritative interpretation of the New Testament – God did not create his Son, as he created the world, but, as Father, generated him from all eternity – proves the divine nature to be something which no philosophy of religion or natural metaphysic could show it to be. (Here we are moving in the realm of the supra-rational mysteries of faith, which, however, are pregnant with rationally exploitable meaning for our natural understanding.) The Creed proves the divine nature to be *essentially self-manifesting fruitfulness* – in which perspective we cannot speak of God as simply 'happening to' create the world, as though this could be fortuitous and uncharacteristic. Delighting to bring into being what is not himself, so as to rejoice in its otherness, is *the* property par excellence which befits the Father's constitution as the first Trinitarian person, what technical theology calls his 'hypostatic particularity'. It is the defining property of the Father that, himself ungenerated and so the primal Source of all that is, he nonetheless generates the eternal Son – and in so doing himself provides the framework of interpretation for his making of the world in time.

Everything we have to say, then, about God as our Creator must be governed by the more primordial truth that he is Father of the Son. It is only in the Son, Jesus Christ, that the Father has revealed who he is in his own essential nature. As Athanasius puts it, to name God 'Father' is not to name some quality in God, but rather, to 'signify his very being'.[116] Only because God is inherently productive – the Greek Fathers employ here words I have already made use of in English equivalents (*gennetikos*, 'generative', *karpogonos*, 'fruitful') – is he the Creator at all.

The relation of the Father to the Son and Spirit

As we have seen, it is because the Father eternally brings forth his Son from within his own being – and not, as with the world, creates him from out of nothing – that the Son, as revelation of the Father, enables us to see the world and humanity within it in a new light: as the typical, not atypical, result of the essential fruitfulness of God. The world is a richly diverse and multifaceted example of that otherness issuing from himself which God loves to love. Belief in the divinity of the Son is thus a necessary condition for finding credible the proposition that God cares passionately for the world (rather than regarding it with a distant and possibly revocable benevolence).

Before considering more fully the divine Son as Son precisely of the Father, I shall pause and interject a comment on the first of my 'disputed questions', and that is the issue raised by Christian feminists as to whether we may regard as mere metaphor, culturally conditioned and hence dispensable, Jesus's designation of his personal Source as Father and the use of the same term by the apostolic Church in naming the ultimate Origin of the salvation given through the Paschal Mystery.

Just as the Christian common sense of those of the Church's faithful who are simultaneously instructed and devout would lead them to find unwarrantable a determination by the Church that use was not to be made – at any rate exclusively – of the name by which Jesus instructed his disciples to address God in prayer (*Abba*, 'Father'), so the theological tradition insists that the term 'Father' is, in Trinitarian language and thought, not a metaphor but a proper name. Already in the Old Testament, the symbolisation of God as 'father' (as in the Canticle of Moses) can be correlated with Israel's sense that God is related to what is in the world by virtue of his very transcendence vis-à-vis the creation.

> A mother goddess is too continuous with the world, too much like the womb from which we came, to stand for the divine reality revealed in the Old Testament, a reality that is decisively other than the world, different from the world, discontinuous with the world, and with a plan, indeed, for the world's remaking . . .[117]

a point which religious feminists of a post-Christian kind, desirous of a different kind of deity, with nature as her body, often unblushingly admit.[118] But in the Gospel, as distinct from the Law and the Prophets, the question is not so much a choice of primary gender symbolism, albeit one made under the constraint of divine inspiration, but the revelation by the eternal Word, now incarnate, of the ultimate divine Origin's proper name. The name of the Father, as that of the Son and of the Holy Spirit, is a 'proper' name. It is *literally* applicable, because it rests on the inter-relation of one divine person to another, and so is not dependent for its justification on an experience of the created medium in the way that some analogically or metaphorically arrived at name for the divine would be. The Father is the principle, the originating starting-point of the Son, as is a human father of the being of his child – and is so in such wise that all earthly fatherhood is but a defective copy of his eternal generation of the Word. Of course, there is no way other than the supernatural by which we could have surmised this: no flesh and blood reveals to us that Christ is thus the Son of the living God. Fortunately for women, and *pace* the Christian feminists, this says nothing at all to the discredit of the Christian and ecclesial dignity of females. As one historian of attitudes to human gender, herself a woman, synthesizes multifarious data here:

> The gender of the deity or leaders of cult does not determine the presence or absence of either religious or social opportunities for either gender.[119]

Now the proper name of Jesus Christ in his relatedness to the Father is Son, and here we must ask why it is of world-shaking significance that Jesus is, as the Creed of Nicaea puts it, *Theos ek Theou*, 'God from God'. Clearly, the question whether or not some human individual is personally identical with the uncreated Word through whom the world was made, can in no circumstances be regarded as a bagatelle. The claim that Jesus of Nazareth was hypostatically united to the Godhead may be dismissed as false, but it can hardly be written off as trivial. Yet put in such terms it remains a question of theory, albeit one of vast speculative importance. The same question when put in the *soteriological* fashion characteristic of the Church's Creeds is charged with existential and practical import for human life and destiny. It is the question, Do the deeds of Jesus Christ as wrought for our salvation have, in the last analysis, only exemplary and morally inspirational value? Or have they actually changed the terms on which the gift of human life is received from God since in those deeds one who was himself personally divine was active precisely so as to re-order the origin, life-resources and final destiny of human beings? The second alternative is the correct one – and why it is vital for the Church to maintain that the incarnate Son has all the prerogatives of God, excepting Fatherhood alone. This she has done by letting her discourse be controlled by that key word *homoousion*, introduced by the bishops at Nicaea. It is an indispensable term, carrying as it does the twofold affirmation that, first, the Son is of identically the same being as the Father (without which he could not save us), and second, the Son is eternally distinct from the Father (without which the divine being could not be known to be endlessly fruitful in itself, and, by dependence on its inherent nature, endlessly fruitful in the free act of our creation). Only

> if Jesus Christ cannot be divided in being and act from God the Father, . . . does he constitute in being and act in his incarnate presence or saving economy the creative self-giving of God to mankind . . .

But since he is *not* so divided, then:

> In virtue of his divine reality and presence incarnate within mankind he acts upon people in an utterly divine and creative way, making them partake of himself through grace and thus partake of God.[120]

As St Irenaeus puts it, knowledge of salvation is simply identical with knowledge of the Son of God *qui et Salus, et Salvator, et Salutare, vere et dicitur et est,* 'who is called and really is "Salvation", and "Saviour", and "Saving Act"',[121] and this because the Son's teaching, deeds and subsequent activity in relation to the faithful *are* the self-revelation and self-communication of the Father.

However, the work of salvation, like the person of the Saviour in his Godward identity, cannot be satisfactorily spoken of without reference to the *Holy Spirit*. Here in the relation of Son to Father and Spirit we come to the second of my disputed questions – though this one, known to historians of doctrine as the *Filioque* dispute, is as ancient in terms of the Christian centuries as the debate over the intrusion of feminism into *sacra doctrina* is modern. In his treatise against the Arians, St Athanasius was obliged to come to terms with those Gospel passages which speak of Christ as somehow indebted to, or dependent on, the Holy Spirit. He interprets them according to the norm of the *homoousion* doctrine, that is, in such a way that they do not in the least diminish what the Father has manifested of his generative power in putting forth his only Son. The Son's indebtedness in his incarnate existence to the Spirit is real yet functional – peculiarly ordered to our salvation. The Word of the Father sanctifies himself in the Spirit *as man* in order that henceforth all human beings may be sanctified in Christ. Thus when at the Baptism in the Jordan, the Spirit descends on the Son made man, this is done, in the words of the great Egyptian doctor 'not for the promotion of the Word himself, but for our sanctification, that we might share in his anointing'.[122] This reluctance to impair the order in which the Trinitarian persons are named in the Church's worship (the doxology runs, 'Glory be to the Father and to the Son and to the Holy Spirit') by introducing theological theses which render the divine being of the Son dependent on the being of the Spirit will finally issue in the doctrine of the Catholic Church that the Spirit's hypostatic particularity lies in his origin not from the Father only but from the Father and the Son. Unfortunately, this is a teaching combatted by a number of Middle and Late Byzantine theologians before and after its dogmatic articulation, as by modern Orthodoxy.

We can note that this problem would never have arisen had it not been for the forthright confession of the Church, East and West, in the eternal Godhead of the Spirit, whose own *homoousion* (consubstantiality with yet distinction from the Father) was the subject matter of the contribution to doctrine of the Second Ecumenical Council, Constantinople I. 'In the Holy Spirit, God acts directly upon us himself, and in giving us his Holy Spirit God gives us nothing less than himself.'[123] In the Spirit the Father reaches out to us through the Word redemptively and sanctifyingly, to bring us into communion with himself. And just as the Son could not save unless he shared fully the divine being and agency that is the Father's, so here it is with the Spirit. In the argument so frequently used by the Cappadocian Fathers against those who queried the Godhead of the Spirit: Only One who is divine can divinise.

The Creed in which the work of those Fathers terminated – the Constantinopolitan recension, and expansion, of the Creed of Nicaea – contents itself with affirming the procession of the Spirit from the Father. It does not add, however, as such Byzantine thinkers as Photius were wont to do, the crucial adverb *monos*: 'from the Father *alone*'. To remove reference to the being of the Son from an account of the being of the Spirit struck some later Easterners as something demanded by fidelity to the letter of the Creed. But at a deeper level it attacks the logical structure implicit in the Creed's making, for it was not through his bringing us some knowledge of the Father independent of the Son that patristic thinkers deemed the Spirit to be one being with the Father, but, on the contrary, owing to the Spirit's activity in revealing the Father in the Son and the Son in the Father. The intention of Byzantine Monopatrism – the theology that would have it that the Spirit is from the Father alone – is a perfectly good one. By contrast with the modern feminism already touched on, it aims to vindicate the Father as fount of the whole Godhead and so of the created world made through the Word by the Breath or Spirit. But it does so by the counter-productive means of denying to the Father that total generosity of fruitful self-giving whereby in generating his Word he gives away to him with the divine nature his (the Father's) property of active spiration. This is the generous act which brings it about that the procession of the Spirit from the Father is – 'as though from a single principle', in the words of the Council of Florence – a procession from the Father and the Son. It is only congruent with the divine fruitfulness – the insight given into the Father's nature by the *homoousion* of the Son – that the Father creatively enables the Son to spirate the Spirit with him. It is, then, for the sake of a deeper congruence between the doctrines of the *homoousion* of Son and of Spirit that the *Filioque* teaching deserves support. And this is an interpretation of its underlying aim that will satisfy those who look to the Greek-speaking doctors of the early centuries for their basic construal of the Gospel.

I said that, in this account of the Father, both in himself and as Source of Son and Spirit, I would consider in passing three controverted issues, and I have yet to mention the last of these, which has no name but consists in a widespread tendency in writing about the Holy Trinity less controlled by the norms of the holy Fathers than that presented here to retroject into a theology of the divine being that attack on the principle of hierarchy so often met with in a democratically minded age in Church and State. Thus whereas an earlier theological style, committed to some form of Trinitarianism but tending to scepticism about how far we can legitimately present a snapshot of, so to speak, the Trinity's home-life, the persons' internal relations of communion, characteristically opted for some form of modalism, treating Father, Son and Spirit as three ways in which the one God presents himself to us as Creator, Redeemer, Sanctifier respectively, it is more typical of a radical theology today to hold to a higher doctrine of the divine persons as persons, but at the same time to dissolve the Trinitarian *taxis*, or order, which has been, historically so important for an appreciation of their inter-relations. Since the idea of the dependence of the second and third persons on the first is deemed to be unacceptably hierarchical – a transgression of that mutuality and exchange which is the hallmark of the relations of communion of Father, Son, and Spirit – the classical accounts of their hierarchically ordered relations of origin are to be abandoned and replaced by a notion of intra-trinitarian 'vitality' in which all the persons are simultaneously co-originating of each other. I will suggest in my conclusion how, once again, this challenge to orthodoxy quite misses the point.

Concealment of the Father: some cultural corollaries

These issues – and the paterological doctrine to which they are a negative response – might seem to be of purely ecclesiastical interest, but the concealing of the true face of the Father can be said to have had ill consequences of a wide-ranging sort in Western culture and society. The death of the divine Father in whom authority and goodness are inseparably united, the font at once of power and value, was proclaimed in the late nineteenth century by Nietzsche not so much as a desideratum in itself but as a necessary condition for the autonomy of man. Revolt against a paternal ancestor was deemed by Freud to be the origin of the projection by psyches in society of images of fatherly divinities that act as foci for guilt-feelings which may sometimes be reality-related but more often belong with psycho-dramas of an irrational kind. Neither Nietzsche nor Freud, the one a child of the manse, the other of the synagogue, ever encountered, we can suppose, the true doctrine of the Father as the ever-generative, fruitful, enabling divine Source, active not in competition with man but for his final flourishing. But the reaction against the Father, however imperfectly grasped, which they pioneered, has produced a society and culture where fathers are instinctively distrusted, where a spirit of unreflective parricide is abroad, where to exercise paternity, by nurture of one's biological children or by formation of one's spiritual children, has become especially difficult. The seething of so many Catholics, influenced by theological or other forms of liberalism and radicalism, when reminded of the names of recent popes is only one obvious example.

That authority should be fatherly is, for this mind-set, only a slightly less egregious error than the assertion that fatherhood – generativity – is essentially authoritative. Resistance to the notion that those who are originative or creative have *eo ipso* some claim to be authority-bearing for others, at any rate in some relevant respect, underlies the current crisis of the 'cultural classic'. The idea that there can be literary texts, or visual artworks, or monuments of thought, or dead people, for that matter, who constitute a kind of authoritative canon of reference in the continuing formation of culture is in many quarters quite as *démodé* as the Father himself. And this also is connected with our theme. For if it is from the Father of lights that all paternity takes its name, then his occlusion will naturally affect not only biological and spiritual but cultural generativity too.

A satisfactory conclusion

The collective trauma created in the Western soul by distortion of the image of the divine Father, followed by murderous revolt against him, can only be healed and pacified by return to its source. And, here is where the best Catholic theology of the twentieth century can help us for it has had recourse, in constructing its Trinitarian doctrine, to the sacrifice of the Cross where it was shown that, while it was the Son who suffered, and the Spirit by whom the Son's oblation was offered, what that oblationary suffering served to reveal was that the Father's nature, from before all time, is itself sacrificial through and through. Thus for the French Benedictine theologian Ghislain Lafont, the 'mysterious face of Fatherhood',[124] which the Father shows by withdrawing into silence at the moment of Jesus's greatest agony, so far from being punitive indifference enables the greatest possible communion between them by opening the maximum space in which the Son made man can abandon himself to the Father. For the influential Swiss dogmatician Hans Urs von Balthasar the Father undergoes a true *kenosis*, or self-emptying, in permitting his beloved Son to enter redemptively into sin and hell, but endures this so that all creation may be reconciled and integrated in the Son's divine-human person. Here the Cross renews in the midst of the creation that self-surrender, *Selbsthingabe*, of the Father to the Son in which his eternal begetting consists.

It is, we can suggest, the *sacrificial* Father who subverts a heterodox feminism, a misguided Mono-patrism, and a false egalitarian anarchism in Trinitarian thinking, just as it is, once again, the Father's sacrifice that must redeem the image of all human fatherhood and its analogues in the life of society and the life of the spirit.

Chapter Five

FOR LIBERAL PROTESTANTS: HOW CHRIST IS PRIEST

Introduction

It is a fundamental Christian conviction that Jesus Christ is no mere inspired teacher, Jewish prophet, rustic sage or Galilaean charismatic – descriptions which may be regarded as typical of liberal Protestant sensibility and scholarship in the various phases of its unfolding. Rather, he is, in his self-presentation, our 'great High Priest' – the title, given him, indeed, within the New Testament Canon, by the Letter to the Hebrews. To grasp what is going on here, the Old Testament background of priesthood is vital, since this is the source from which, in biblical revelation and Christian tradition, the language of priesthood arises. Old Testament priesthood furnishes the point of reference when, in Hebrews, Jesus is called our great High Priest. A Jesus deprived of this dimension can still teach and even work miracles. But why he should be acclaimed by the Church a divine-human Redeemer is, on the truncated reading typical of liberal or radical exegesis, much less clear.

A key principle

Though the Letter to the Hebrews is, of course, the great testimony to the Priesthood of Christ in the New Testament, I am keen to support those who would not leave it in splendid isolation in this regard. To consider a priestly Christology the sole preserve of the Writer to the Hebrews might be to suggest this could be something of a 'sport' in the Canon, which could conceivably be sidelined without great loss. What a contrast with, for example, the Christology of St Thomas Aquinas for which the Priesthood of Christ as mediator between God and humankind is absolutely central and constitutive. The importance of the category of Christ's High Priesthood in the classical theology of Western Catholicism makes me sympathetic to those exegetes, often non-Catholic, who seek to rescue this same category from the near-oblivion to which 'higher criticism' of the Gospels and 'Life of Jesus research', usually on liberal Protestant presuppositions, have by and large abandoned it.

In approaching the Old Testament (and, for that matter, inter-Testamental) evidence, we need to respect a more general principle which was well articulated by the twelfth-century theologian Hugh of Saint-Victor in his treatise 'On the Sacraments of the Christian Faith'. Ever since the Fall of man, God has put in place what Hugh calls *sacramenta* – I translate that 'working signs' – designed for the purpose of human salvation.[125] Throughout the various epochs of the history of salvation, the object of faith always remains the same, the Creator God and the redeeming Christ,[126] such that both the regime of nature, under paganism, and the epoch of the Old Covenant have certain *sacramenta* of the Coming One.[127] Indeed, the Old Covenant has an entire saving economy of 'precepts, working signs, and promises' although, as Hugh stresses, these require retrospective theological elucidation for their right understanding.[128] Possibly it is this Victorine background which explains why St Thomas gives so lengthy and detailed an account of the Old Law.[129] Israel's religion is, Thomas explains, a divine 'disposition' of things which constitutes a preparation and prefiguration of the New Law, all held within the unity of God's saving plan.[130]

This means that pertinent to our subject are Old Testament concepts and practices of priesthood – in both the Levitical/Aaronic stream, which comes from the Mosaic tradition, paramount in Israel, and also the stream flowing from the figures of Melchizedek and Zadok, interest in whom was strongest in the Davidic and Zion traditions, centred in Jerusalem.[131] In the Hebrew Bible, priesthood – the mediation of the divine to the human, the human to the divine – goes back deep into the Mosaic origins of Israel's faith. Aaron, the brother of Moses, is the first high priest, and the sons of Aaron remain a priestly family *par excellence* while the menfolk of the entire tribe of Levi are deputed for priestly duties. Again, at Jerusalem in particular, Jews did not forget the figure of Melchizedek, the mysterious priest-king of Salem who gave his blessing to Abraham, the fore-father of the people of God.[132] Zadok was also important to them. Included in the genealogies from Aaron and Levi in the Books of Chronicles,[133] he was the Jerusalem priest (a spiritual link with Melchizedek – note the similarity of name – is probable) who, at David's request, anointed Solomon king.[134] In the restored Temple seen by the prophet Ezekiel in his vision, only the 'sons of Zadok' may minister.[135] Such Israelite institutions, and the texts that recall them, are covered by the apostle's teaching that all Scripture (the entire Old Testament) serves for our 'instruction' as Christians.[136] In the words of the seventeenth-century spiritual theologian M. Olier:

> God has ordained nothing in the ancient Law which he has not related to what his Son was to be and do in the Church.[137]

The key to the relation of the Testaments is, accordingly, the notion of a surpassing fulfilment – a 'super-fulfilment', for both noun and adjective are necessary. And this gives us in turn a 'principle of prefiguration' whereby persons, events and, not least, institutions from the Old Testament can enjoy a positive significance vis-à-vis the New. I take that to be the key principle that should guide us in scanning the biblical background to the New Testament texts and events. Readers of my third apologia, 'For academic exegetes: reading Scripture in the Church', will not be surprised. In its light, I now formulate a septet of inter-related Christological claims on the New Testament's behalf.

The expectation of a priestly Messiah

My first claim is that, in the Providence of God, the *expectation of a priestly Messiah* – a Messiah who would exercise in supreme fashion the Old Testament priesthood surveyed above – belongs with the historical particularities of the Incarnation. That expectation has, so we shall see, a fitting reflection in Jesus's ministry.

The Qumran literature (the 'Dead Sea Scrolls'), along with that rather earlier discovery the 'Damascus Document', make it plain that, in the period between the Old and New Testaments, eschatological expectation included the awaiting of a priestly Messiah, 'The Anointed One of Aaron', and not only a royal Messiah, 'The Anointed One of Israel'. The self-same expectation is found in the contemporary text entitled the *Testaments of the Twelve Patriarchs*.[138] A figure is awaited who will sum up the priesthood not only of Aaron but of Melchizedek as well. One text in the Dead Sea Scrolls celebrates in fact the prospective return of Melchizedek to rescue his people from the power of the Evil One.[139] People were looking, evidently, for a super-fulfilment of what the Old Testament contains. True, such 'inter-Testamental' literature is not covered by the charism of biblical inspiration, exclusive as this is to the books of the Canon.[140] But that doesn't mean to say it can't form part of the providential disposition of things for the mission of the eternal Son in historical time.

The formulaic title 'Holy One of God', given to

Jesus in St Mark's Gospel,[141] and picked up again in the Gospel of St John,[142] has overtones of just such a figure. Old Testament priests were said to be 'consecrated to their God',[143] while the high priest was to wear on his turban a plate inscribed with similar words.[144] Familiar elements in the ministry of Jesus like his exorcisms, declarations of pardon, blessing of children, can easily be associated with the exercise of priesthood.[145] These elements will not, however, fall readily into a pattern of this kind unless the reader takes up the perspective of *looking out for super-fulfilment*, the matching of the evidence with providentially generated expectations. Hence, of course, the limited support this thesis has found among exegetes who fail to recognize the importance of the general principle involved. By contrast, Hugh of Saint-Victor's principle is taken for granted by those who accept the unity of Scripture, as read in the Church.

Priestly Intercessor for the disciples

My second claim takes us from Jesus's public ministry to the circumstances of his death. In Jesus's Farewell Discourse he acts as *priestly Intercessor for the disciples* while he prepares for his saving sacrifice. The developed theology of Christ's Priesthood in Hebrews, by linking such Priesthood above all to his Passion, death and exaltation, encourages us to seek further evidence for an implicit sense of the Priesthood of Christ in the Passion narratives (as well as from the Resurrection appearances – of which the Ascension is, in its own highly distinctive way, the last). The role of priestly intercession in that 'discourse' on the first Holy Thursday flags up for us the priestly task Jesus took on supremely in his dying.

In the Farewell Discourse, which forms the prelude to the Passion narrative of the Gospel of St John, chapter 17 enjoys a very marked liturgical character. With good reason it has acquired the title 'The High Priestly Prayer'. While that title seems to have emerged in later sixteenth-century Lutheranism, what it signifies was long recognized. Thus, for instance, among the mediaeval divines, abbot Rupert of Deutz writes of this section of St John's Gospel, '[He who is] Priest and Sacrifice prayed for us'.[146]

Public intercession is already, for the tradition of Israel, a priestly activity. But more specifically, Jesus's prayer is for the perfecting of the unity of the disciples, a unity whose source and model is that of the Father and the Son. This prayer picks up – precisely by the way it stresses unity – the theme of the Allegory of the Vine, with its overtones of Eucharistic wine. This is a parable Jesus has just taught the disciples, in solemn tones.[147] The perfected unity that is the object of his intercessory action is bound up, so it seems, with communion in the Holy Eucharist, the sacrament of the saving Sacrifice shortly to be offered.[148] This suggests how in the High Priestly Prayer the Priesthood of Christ is *together with intercession, sacrificial offering*. My 'third claim' takes this proposal further.

The sacrificial Offering

My third claim runs: the Last Supper involves a *sacrificial offering* by the new High Priest. Though the setting of the institution of the Eucharist is an actual (or, possibly, anticipated) Passover, Jesus uses the opportunity to put in place a new rite which has resonances of other aspects of Israelite ritual. It has echoes of the peace-offering whose first celebration was the sealing of the Sinai covenant.[149] It is also reminiscent of the atonement rites of Yom Kippur.[150] Generally speaking, the peace-offering was not considered to atone for sins. Accordingly, Matthew's account of the Last Supper can be thought to contain an allusion, in the words of institution – 'my Blood of the Covenant which is poured out for many for the remission of sins'[151] – to the high priest's pouring out of blood at the climax of the ritual of the Day of Atonement.[152] As Dr Margaret Barker explains, on that awesome day:

> in a state of absolute purity, the high priest went into the holy of holies, to the heart of space and time, and there . . . sprinkled blood, i.e. life. This was the turning of the year, the rite of renewal, the turning of history.[153]

The many-sidedness of the ritual practice and rhetoric of the Old Testament allows us to include here likewise – through that key phrase *'for many'* of the institution formula – a reference to the prophet Isaiah's 'Suffering Servant'. In those famous oracles in the Book of Isaiah, we hear, like the Church in Holy Week, of one who offered vicariously the sacrifice of himself for the sake of the multitude. In the last of the Servant Songs,[154] the Servant makes of his own person a sin offering and offers it, and in so doing takes on a priestly role.

> The use of cultic language makes it clear what the prophet is thinking: what the expiatory victims offered in the temple by the Israelite clergy cannot accomplish, the Servant wins from God, because "he was bearing the faults of many and praying all the time for sinners".[155]

Insofar as Jesus recognized himself in the mysterious figure of the Servant, he implicitly presented himself as Priest of the New Covenant.[156] Indeed, insofar as he saw himself as *combining* in his own person the gloriously transcendent 'Son of Man' of the Book of Daniel and the humble 'Servant of the Lord' of the Book of Isaiah, he implicitly presented himself as the *divine*-human Priest of that covenant.

In the Passion, the transcendent Son of Man becomes the Servant. In the Farewell Discourse, this is acted out, in sign and foretaste, when he washes the disciples' feet. He is to offer his life in sacrifice. In both regards – Servant, Son of Man – we are dealing with transformations of the Messianic idea whose upshot is a priestly act, an act that cries out for interpreting in priestly terms. 'Christ loved us and gave himself up for us, a fragrant offering and sacrifice to God'.[157] With this we can compare the key phrase in the High Priestly Prayer, 'For their sake I consecrate myself'.[158] The union of intercession with sacrificial offering forms the culminating action in the ministry of the Servant who is also the Son of Man.

Changing the veil and vesture

My fourth claim is more speculative. It is also rather fascinating. The Passion of Christ in the Synoptics entails the *replacement of the veil and vesture of the ancient priesthood*. All the Synoptics[159] record the tearing of the temple veil at the moment of the redeeming death. Margaret Barker calls this a 'graphic illustration of the identity of [Christ's] flesh and [temple] veil'.[160] What does she mean?

The veil which, *architecturally speaking*, separated the temple hall from the inner sanctum, the holy of holies, also separated, *symbolically speaking*, earth from heaven. In Israel's liturgy, it was, precisely, the high priest who could move, ritually speaking, in and out through the veil. In coming out through the veil, he wore vestments made of the same fabrics and colours as the veil itself,[161] thus indicating the intimate connexion between the veil and the high priest's person. The replacement of the veil implies nothing less than the *coming of a new High Priest*.

But if the Temple veil is significant, then so too are the high priestly garments. In the accounts given by Jewish commentators of the time of Jesus,[162] the colours of the high priest's vestments represent the cosmic elements, which helps to explain the claim of the book of Wisdom that 'upon [Aaron's] long robe the whole world was depicted'.[163] The high priest was dressed not just in (as we say in an English expression) 'all the colours of the rainbow'. He was clothed in all the colours of the cosmos. And conversely, for the same commentators, when the high priest entered the holy of holies, he wore white vestments, suitable to the angelic world of the court of God which he visited in the symbolic heaven where he had been praying.

Apply this to Jesus, and we find a theologically sumptuous parallel. If Christ the Priest took to himself the cosmic elements in the garment of flesh he assumed at the Incarnation,[164] the same Christ wore a dazzlingly white robe in the Synoptic accounts of the Transfiguration, itself an anticipation of the Resurrection and Ascension events.[165] By his Easter triumph, the Jesus who, in his divine nature, never left the true Holy of Holies – the Father's side – entered there in his human nature in a definitive way for the first time.

The Ascension as priestly blessing

In my fifth claim, the Ascension is the *priestly blessing* by Christ of the members of the nascent Church. In the final Christophany of St Luke's Gospel, the ascending Jesus, before withdrawing into the world beyond the veil, gives the disciples a solemn blessing.[166] Compare that priestly blessing of Abraham by Melchizedek already mentioned,[167] and note how, in the book of Sirach, Simon Maccabeus gives a blessing as high priest in a comparable fashion.[168]

At the end of Luke's Gospel this blessing serves to indicate the Christological foundation for the descent on the apostles of the Holy Spirit at the opening of the sequel, the Book of Acts. As events will show, it is an 'epicletic' blessing, one that calls down the Spirit of God. The structure of the Church's worship, borne as it is by the dual missions of Christ and the Spirit, will reflect this climactic moment. In adoring the Father, the Church becomes a Spirit-filled house 'through Christ our Lord'.

Jesus fulfils the figure of Melchizedek

According to my sixth claim, Jesus *fulfils the figure of Melchizedek*. If the figure of the priest (or high priest or priest-king) was important for Jesus's environment, and, so the above references suggest, for Jesus himself and his canonical witnesses in the evangelists and St Paul, it is hardly surprising that the Letter to the Hebrews – from where this apologia started! – takes up the titles 'great High Priest' and 'Priest for ever, according to the order of Melchizedek'. That is so, above all, in chapter 7 of the Letter where the superiority of Melchizedek's priesthood over its Levitical counterpart is argued for in a way which simultaneously suggests how Melchizedek bears a 'resemblance' to the Son of God.[169]

For the Writer to the Hebrews, the Old Testament cultus could not of itself attain its goal. That goal had been twofold. It was meant, first, to carry human worship to God. Alas, it did not bring God a worship he could accept.[170] It was meant, secondly, to sanctify men by relating them to him. Sadly, it was powerless to purify them from their sins and make them 'perfect'.[171] By contrast, the sacrifice of our great High

Priest Jesus Christ satisfied both these aims.

> The intervention of Christ . . . , the manner in which, through his passion, he established himself in a new relationship with God and with mankind – this entire intervention has effectively achieved all that the Old Testament sacrifices aspired to do. . . . This is why the action of Christ must be recognized as priestly and must be called a "sacrifice". For this reason, one must be careful not to say that the author of the Epistle is using 'metaphors' when he applies the title of high priest to Christ and the name of "sacrifice" to his glory-producing passion. [The author's] viewpoint is exactly the opposite: it is in the Old Testament that priesthood and sacrifice were taken in the metaphorical sense, as they are there applied to an impotent and symbolic figuration, while in the mystery of Christ these words have at last obtained their real meaning, with an unsurpassed completeness.[172]

In this manner of defining the relation between the two Testaments, the contrast between shadow and (heavenly or eschatological) reality underlines above all the imperfection of the Elder Covenant and attests its definitive surpassing. Yet there is, between the one and the other, a profound unity and continuity, so much so that the second 'fulfils' – in our terms, 'super-fulfils' - the first.

The sub-apostolic age will register this stupendous change, taking up the theme of the unique and definitive Priesthood, not only with regard to Christ's Sacrifice, but to the entirety of his ministry, including his teaching office. As Ignatius of Antioch wrote, 'To Jesus alone as our high priest were the secret things of God committed . . .',[173] 'secret things' which provided the substance of his teaching and the saving plan he embodied as Messianic priest-king. In its emphasis on the priesthood of Christ, the Letter to the Hebrews stands, I suggest, in a wider tradition that courses through the first centuries of the Christian era from its fountain-head in Jesus himself.[174]

The true Priest-King

Finally, then, in a seventh and last claim, Jesus is the *true Priest-King,* fulfilment of the messianic hope. Such a view of the fulfilment of the messianic hope can fit into the claims of the Davidide heir, that more familiar theme of the royal Messiah, and need not compete with them. The bifurcation of Messiah-hood into priestly and royal is a distinction within a wider unity. In Israel's sacral monarchy, Zion theology gave the king a certain priestly quality, as witness Psalm 110 (109), whose setting in life would seem to be the enthronement of a Davidic king, but which declares him 'a priest for ever after the order of Melchizedek'.[175] In the Synoptic tradition, Jesus applies to himself just that psalm where the Messiah is both king and priest.[176] As once, in the Hasmonaean period, immediately before the dynasty of Herod when the Babe of Bethlehem was born, high priesthood and royalty had been united in the same person, so now they came to be united again, but in unutterably transformed mode, in Jesus Christ.

The difference between Jesus and the sacred rulers of Israel is obvious. What in Psalm 110 was said of the latter *ritually* – 'You are my son, today I have begotten you'[177] – this divine declaration was true of Jesus *not just in symbolic speech or action but in all reality*. The divine Son who actually *was* generated eternally became in historical time the royal High Priest who would bring finite and guilty men into the divine presence – bring us into meta-history, into the everlasting presence of God.

That Jesus was and is a Priest – *the* Priest for the human race, his priesthood now invested in the Church and ministry that bear his name – is an apologia Catholic Christians must not fail to offer.

Chapter Six

FOR PROGRESSIVE CATHOLICS: THE COUNCIL AND THE GOSPEL OF LIFE

Introduction

One of the jewels in the crown of the Catholic priesthood in England is an 'Association of Priests for the Gospel of Life'. That is not only a beautiful idea in the Church at any time. It is also a necessary idea in the Church in our country at the present time. It is principally necessary owing to the moral wasteland into which England has fallen. But it is necessary in a secondary way because when considering the moral condition of culture, members of the Church have not always sent out clear signals to the people of our day. And that is inappropriate to a nation called to be, through the grace of the New Covenant mediated by the Saviour, themselves a 'kingdom of priests'.

So by way of introduction I would like to say a word about these two somewhat inter-connected states of affairs. First, what I call, with apologies to T. S. Eliot, the wasteland. How can we characterise the moral culture which surrounds us? It is a culture of individual rights coexisting with a high degree of scepticism about the distinction between right and wrong, and a retreat from responsibility. To a degree it already was these things in Eliot's day, but the degree in question has since been grossly maximised. A sample of instances of contemporary moral anarchy pertinent to life-issues suggests how much. By the year 2020 on present trends in the United Kingdom, married couples will be a minority, and one in three people will be living alone – with all the implications that must have for the procreation and nurture of children. Again: it can be reported with no expectation of outrage that a lesbian couple practising self-insemination before breaking up their partnership had two Do-It-Yourself babies using a pickle jar and syringe, and another similar couple purchased the frozen sperm of a stranger via the Internet.[178] Yet again: to test the potential curative powers of human embryonic stem cells, biologists are currently seeking to inject them into laboratory animals so that, to take two examples of proposed experiments by scientists in good standing in their profession, a mouse might have a brain made up entirely of human cells, a chimpanzee might have a human mid-brain spliced into its own with the consequence, it is predicted, that though unable to talk, it would be able to laugh or at least sob.[179] Faced with the issues raised by such a sampling of scenarios and others of less directly pro-life concern, there can be noted, reports the ethical commentator David Selbourne, eleven types of evasive argument, which he lists as follows: the notion that 'there is nothing you can do about it, or not much'; the idea that 'it has never been any different'; the proposition that 'there is no quick fix' for a given ethical dilemma; the excuse that 'this is the price of a free society'; the call that 'everything is changing and you must move with the tide'; the cliché that 'it is no use turning the clock back'; the insistence that a problem is 'much more complex than you think'; the alibi that a problem is 'beyond the reach of law'; the objection that 'you are focusing on the wrong issue'; the defence that 'people in glass houses shouldn't . . .'; and, basest of all, since 'everyone does it, or most-people-do', how can you object?[180]

As Selbourne points out, the overall effect of these evasions is to paralyse debate, but if the arguer persists he or she will as likely as not be dismissed as a 'moral crusader', a 'moral authoritarian', a 'puritan', or, as he puts it, 'the old standby – "right-wing"'.[181] As the Chief Rabbi of Great Britain has put it:

> A view has slowly coalesced that the individual makes choices and the State deals with the consequences of those choices without passing judgment. Order is guaranteed [he goes on] by the police, education by the national curriculum, welfare by government agencies. Morality – the acquisition of habits of self-restraint – has become redundant.[182]

What, then, about my second introductory motif, the sending-out of signals by Catholics nationally to their non-Catholic contemporaries about the moral scene? I am not thinking here of official statements – by 2004 at any rate, with the Catholic Bishops

Conference booklet *Cherishing Life*, these had become savvy – but of unofficial attitudes among a tranche of ordinary laity and clergy, and of the not-so-ordinary would-be opinion-formers in the media. As so often, those attitudes were affected by the confusion into which Catholic teaching fell in England, if not only here, in the immediate aftermath of the Council, as also by the desire, in a national church (if the phrase may be allowed) emerging from the ghetto, to capture the benevolence of the wider public. I think it is fair to say that from the later 1960s on such responses frequently took the form of what might be called 'attenuated existentialism'.

Attenuated existentialism, while not necessarily denying in a formal way the reality of an abiding human nature, or the ethical demands integral to the order of grace, nonetheless emphasised chiefly the sincerity of those involved in moral decision-making, and the authenticity of decisions made according to personal conscience. When people say, 'But it's my right', they are, it was and is felt, staking out a proper claim to due autonomy which should be respected, whatever the so-called 'Yuck factor' involved. The Church, after all, following the example of her Master, should not sit in judgment on the world, but serve it, statements which can claim some corroboration from the Pastoral Constitution of the Second Vatican Council on the Church in the Modern World, *Gaudium et spes*, since its preface ends with more or less exactly those words.

I shall be looking at some strengths and weaknesses

of that document in our perspective in a moment. But let me for now contrast what I have called the 'attenuated existentialism' of secular-minded Catholic liberalism with two citations coming from (as they say) somewhere very different. The first is taken from the writings of the historian of philosophy Etienne Gilson, and considers one crucial theme already touched on, namely conscience:

> Besides being bound to obey our conscience [wrote Gilson], we are also bound, whenever an error of judgment is to be feared, to criticize it, and to replace a bad conscience by a better.[183]

The second citation is pertinent to the wider question of Church strategy, and it has no less a source than the founder of *The Tablet*, Frederick Lucas. Lucas asked:

> What principles can beget and develop enthusiasm for the cause of the Church? . . . Is it by acting so as to satisfy and please the half-religious, the indifferent, the careless, the timid, that men can ever create religious (or other) enthusiasm? Is it by truckling to fears, and doubts, and deficient energy? Was it by half-measures that St Paul inspired his followers with a willingness to die? Was it by meeting the wisdom of the world half-way that Hildebrand saved the Church from its oppressors? [And he replied to his own questions:] We think not.[184]

The hermeneutic of renewal in continuity

I feel moderately certain that this phrase will be more than a polysyllabic exotic to some readers. It was in fact popularised (if that is indeed the word) by the present Pope in an address to the Roman Curia on the 40th anniversary of the conclusion of the Second Vatican Council: 22nd December, 2005. That address sought to define one way of reading the texts of that Council as the only way fully acceptable within the context of Catholic tradition. But, by its emphasis on continuity rather than rupture as the hallmark of the Spirit's guidance in Tradition (in 'tradition' there, a capital T is called for), Benedict's speech also exemplified a wider mind-set in Christian thinking. In some pithy words of G. K. Chesterton:

> [r]eal development is not leaving things behind, as on a road, but drawing life from them, as from a root.[185]

Treating the Conciliar moment as one of reform not revolution, Benedict XVI spoke of the proper method of appropriating the Conciliar texts as a hermeneutic suited to such reform, which implies, as he put it:

> renewal in the continuity of the one subject-Church that the Lord has given to us. She is a subject that increases in time and develops; yet always remaining the same, the one subject of the journeying People of God.

Oddly enough, the Pope was, I think, more eloquent or at any rate more fulsome on the topic of the hermeneutic of discontinuity which he was opposing. Typically, he declared, the practititioners of such a hermeneutic claim that the texts of the Council

are the result of compromises in which, to reach

unanimity, it was found necessary to keep and reconfirm many old things that are now pointless. However, the true spirit of the Council is not [it was alleged] to be found in these compromises but instead in the impulses toward the new that are contained in the texts. These innovations alone were supposed to represent the true spirit of the Council, and starting from and in conformity with them, it would be possible to move ahead. Precisely because the texts would only imperfectly reflect the true spirit of the Council and its newness, it would be necessary to go courageously beyond the texts and make room for the newness in which the Council's deepest intention would be expressed, even if it were still vague. In a word: it would be necessary not to follow the texts of the Council but its spirit. In this way, obviously [the Pope argued], a vast margin was left open for the question of how this spirit should subsequently be defined and room was consequently made for every whim.

All this, commented the Pope, exemplified a failure to grasp the nature of the conciliar process. An Ecumenical Council is not a constituent assembly that, as he put it, 'eliminates an old constitution and creates a new one'. As he concluded:

The Fathers [i.e. the bishops in Council] had no such mandate and no one had ever given them one; nor could anyone have given them one because the essential constitution of the Church comes from the Lord and was given to us so that we might attain eternal life and, starting from this perspective, be able to illuminate life in time and time itself.[186]

I think it is worth reminding ourselves of this important interpretative principle, even at the expense of so lengthy a citation, since in order to claim for the proclamation of the Gospel of life a non-ambiguous mandate in the documents of the Council, we need to be able to clear away the misunderstanding whereby what I termed 'attenuated existentialism' could stand as a legitimate expression of Vatican II's attitude towards moral culture at large.

Am I setting up here a straw man to be too easily knocked down? Has anyone actually held that 'attenuated existentialism' *is* the implicit recommended stance towards other persons in civil society of the Church at Vatican II? Well, no – though that is partly because I've only just come up with the expression! What *has* been discerned in the small or not so small print of *Gaudium et spes* is, however, two claims which, taken together, would generate an attitude very much like the one I have described. Stating these two claims takes us into the meat of the Pastoral Constitution. Responding to them on the basis of a fuller reading of the Conciliar text, against the backcloth of Tradition with, in the foreground, some declarations of the post-Conciliar papal magisterium in mind, will help us, I hope, to answer convincingly the claim that what the Association of Priests for the Gospel of Life is doing may represent the priorities of Karol Wojtyła and his personal theological preoccupation with, in his own phrase, the 'culture of death', but it does not have much to do with the last General Council of the Church.

Reading 'Gaudium et spes'

The two claims made by interpreters of the Pastoral Constitution which, once read in tandem, could appear to license attenuated existentialism are these. First, at certain points – such as paragraphs 36 and 59 – *Gaudium et spes* asserts the autonomy vis-à-vis the Church of the secular sciences, of human culture, and of civil society at large. While some commentators, like the contributors to the Alberigo *History of Vatican II*, reacted with at any rate equanimity,[187] others, like Dr Tracey Rowland of the John Paul II Institute in Melbourne, were absolutely aghast.[188] Historians can note in an eirenic kind of way that, doubtless, many of the bishops were seeking to reassure scientists, artists, professionals and politicians that the Church after the Council would not wish to maintain or re-institute a heavy-handed or overbearing style of ecclesiastical regime. But the question remains, Do such presentational concerns suffice to explain the wording of what are, after all, doctrinal texts, or should one say, as one reader of Rowland's book puts it:

> that the Council fathers overreacted to the threat of integralism because they had already grown weary of the baggage of the Church's tradition in general and desired to throw off some of the weight and ballast of the past in order to embrace a liberal order for which many of them had deep sympathies.[189]

In point of fact, Rowland does not think that things were that bad. But she does think that by embracing at certain points of their text notions of moral and cultural autonomy the Council fathers were extraordinarily naive. They failed to realise that, in the way modern culture has developed, that culture is not neutral vis-à-vis the *bona recepta*, the 'received goods' – truths, values, practices – of Catholic Christianity. Far less is it likely to serve as a *praeparatio evangelica* in the way classical culture did. Unfortunately, statements can also be found – not, thank goodness, uniformly – from the popes of the Council which give the impression that, as Professor Larry Chapp of DeSales University, Pennsylvania, has it, modern culture might embody in a secular way

> many of the same truths held by the Church in a more theological modality, thus opening the door to a new level of cooperation between the secular and ecclesiological realms, as well as implying a general approval for the manner in which modern secularism had developed culturally.[190]

The first ground, then, for asserting a basis for attenuated existentialism in the Pastoral Constitution lies in the licence it gives at various points to the sciences, culture and society in general to develop in their own fashion in fulfilment of their rightful claims to autonomy. As early as 1969 one Joseph Ratzinger could be found deploring what he deemed the Pelagian overtones of such autonomy discourse. Actually, what he said was rather stronger than that: *Gaudium et spes* was marred by *eine geradezu pelagianische Terminologie*, 'a thoroughly Pelagian terminology'.[191] Certainly the language used by the Council fathers was a far cry from John Paul II's reported practice in *ad limina* visits of asking bishops what they were doing to 'change culture' in their countries.

The second ground for asserting such a basis for attenuated existentialism is connected with the issue of the manner in which modern secularism has developed culturally. And this has to do not so much with particular brief paragraphs, or the odd sentence, in the document. It concerns, rather its overall theological framework which, it is alleged, considers man to be first and foremost the creative animal destined for global dominion, whose dignity lies in his capacity to imitate, and indeed participate in, the creativity of God by achieving effective mastery over the world – thus paragraph 12 of *Gaudium et spes* which is the Constitution's initial statement about the dignity of human persons.

Put that together with the occasional assertions about the autonomy of the secular and what might we get? Is not what we might get the idea that human intervention in the created order through the ingenuity of technology, including medical technology, is in and of itself (no further questions asked) an example of human beings acting exactly as they should, namely, in the image of God who is absolute and intrinsic creativity as distinct from our contingent and mediated creativity? In that case, the message of the text, is, not to put too fine a point on it, the message of the serpent in the Garden: *sicut dii eritis*, 'Ye shall be as gods'. It is the anthropological error known to students of European literature as Prometheanism from the Greek hero Prometheus who stole fire from the gods and brought it down to earth. If we follow this view of the overall theological framework in *Gaudium et spes* – which means in terms of the text privileging the rather theistic-sounding, as distinct from Trinitarian, statement in paragraph 12 over a densely Christological correlative statement in paragraph 22 – then, to cite Chapp again:

> The emphasis will be on human doing and can lead, ironically, to an almost Promethean spirituality that views it as our theological imperative to take on duties that have traditionally been ascribed to the agency of God – as seen for example in the instrumentalization of human life in abortion and embryo research – all justified by liberal Christians on the grounds that God has blessed us with rationality and it is now our duty to creatively subdue the world by bringing everything, including human life itself, under the umbrella of the technological imperative.[192]

It was, I think I am correct in saying, John Paul II, in his first encyclical, *Redemptor Hominis*, who was the first to highlight the importance, rather, of the alternative *imago Dei* doctrine in *Gaudium et spes*, the Christologically ordered one, as a more adequate key, against the background of Tradition, to the message of the Pastoral Constitution as a whole. But, taking up this cue, it was a Washington theologian, David

Schindler, a Balthasarian and the editor of the English-language version of the journal *Communio*, who most fully drew out the implications – crucially in an important article in *Communio* for 1996,[193] but at greater length in his book of the same year, *Heart of the World*, whose sub-title includes, significantly, the words 'liberalism and liberation'.[194] Schindler's claim was that if, in the light of *Gaudium et spes* 22, one adopts for reading the document – and for doctrine at large – a more Christologically oriented anthropology, then the primary constitutive act of human agency shifts from one of active creativity to one of an active receptivity of creation: active receptivity of creation as sheer gift. If I am the image of God by reference to the Trinitarian Son, then *receiving* – as the Son does from the Father – is more crucial for me, more primordial (in Schindler's term, more *constitutive*) than any creative action I might perform. Indeed, it is, wrote Schindler, the 'inner-anterior condition of all creaturely doing and making'.[195] This 'receiving' in my case, as an image of *the* Image, the Son, means receiving first and foremost from God in his creation of myself. By my nature I am not a god. I am not even like unto a god. Instead, I am a gift. Such awareness of the 'giftedness' of existence will naturally extend beyond 'mere gratitude for my own existence into an appreciation of the giftedness of the existence of the "other".' This alternative anthropology will, therefore, appropriately issue in an 'ethic of love rather than one of manipulative domination'.[196]

In those last words we are coming within hailing

distance of a 'Gospel of life', but what I want us to draw from this debate is also an inkling of how an emphasis on the potency of the human person, acting in the place of the Creator, especially where that action has access to modern technology, notably medical technology, could easily – and disastrously – fuse with an emphasis on autonomy – scientific autonomy, cultural autonomy, civil autonomy – to produce precisely an ethic of manipulative domination totally untutored by the teaching and ethos of the Church, and totally untutored, above all, by her great narrative of how her Lord and Master became our redeemer in the womb of blessed Mary and manifested his power of love at its uttermost in his physical weakness when dying on the Cross – with all the pregnant implications these Christological episodes have for the issues of abortion and euthanasia. It is not hard to see how, at a less sophisticated conceptual level, and tempered no doubt by habitual charity, what ordinary Church people drew from such a fusion of Prometheanism and autonomy-thinking was some version of what I've been terming 'attenuated existentialism', itself a mild form of the overall stance of contemporary modernity in the secular setting.

For many people the controversy aroused by *Humanae Vitae* took this hitherto fitfully crystallising attitude and fixed it in amber. The alternative to allowing what were really secular *mores* some ecclesial space was just too provocative, too painful, too divisive. Any search for common ground with secular modernity can only be, however, a highly ambiguous good for the

Church, simply because if the foundational principle of that modernity is Promethean autonomy (and this seems likely) then such modernity can only be *au fond* anti-Christian. It's hardly surprising that in the contemporary West the view that religion should be in this or that regard determinative of secular activities has come to be deemed, as Cardinal Avery Dulles put it, no better than fanaticism.[197] Nor does that opinion simply postdate '9/11'.

So far, I may have given the impression that *Gaudium et spes* is at least equally amenable to interpretations that point towards and away from classical Christianity – or maybe is, taken neat, more susceptible than not to a discontinuous or revolutionary hermeneutic. In the areas that concern us, such a hermeneutic would, in context, enfeeble Gospel of life imperatives by defining human dignity in the typically liberal terms of autonomy of choice: 'pro-choice' as the phrase has it. In that case, the list of anti-life infamies in paragraph 27 of the Constitution would be an example of what Pope Benedict in his 2005 address called standard reiterations of ancient teaching which pale into insignificance compared with the innovatory impulses in the text which are what is really interesting about it. Despite the weaknesses in *Gaudium et spes* (I take it we have gone beyond the stage of Conciliar fundamentalism which can admit no flaws at all in the Council's wording), that is hardly the message of the text.

It is worth going through the Pastoral Constitution with the following question in mind: In what, for *Gaudium et spes*, does human dignity consist? It is plain that the answer cannot simply be autonomous choice since the document speaks of the need not only to recognise human dignity but to elevate and perfect it (for example in paragraphs 17 and 19). For such perfecting it seeks education of mind and purification of the heart (for instance in paragraph 14). At various points it emphasises the building of moral character through the cultivation of the virtues and the extirpation of the vices. At paragraph 40 it speaks of the Church's 'healing and elevating impact' on the dignity of the person. It does not sell out to the characteristically Modern, whether liberal or Marxian, position that justice is best established not through the formation of just persons (the view of the ancients from Plato to St Thomas More) but by putting in place the most appropriate structures and procedures in society. This personal justice must surely be in mind when the Constitution says in paragraph 26 that freedom must be founded on truth, built on justice and animated by love: it is hard to see how structures and procedures can be said to *love* – of all things. *Gaudium et spes* stresses that people must exercise their rights in the light of the moral law or they will diminish their dignity. Thus paragraph 41:

> We are tempted to think that our personal rights are fully ensured only when we are exempt from every requirement of divine law. But this way lies not the maintenance of the dignity of the human person, but its destruction.

Indeed, in paragraph 43 we learn how the 'well-formed

Christian conscience' has to see to it that 'the divine law is inscribed in the life of the earthly city'. And more widely, through allusions scattered throughout the body of the text, it is possible to assemble from the Pastoral Constitution the summary of the threefold ground of human dignity later given by John Paul II in *Christifideles laici:* created in God's image and likeness, redeemed by Jesus Christ, destined for eternal life in communion with God.[198]

Conclusion

Gilson, whom I've already quoted, considered that the changeover in the patristic world from pagan to Christian ethics consists precisely in adding such theocentric reference to a description of the life of the virtues.

> They [the Christians] regarded the soul of a just man as beautiful and worthy of honour because virtuous, but virtue itself as honourable only because it leads to God. It is therefore not the supreme good, the *nec plus ultra*, that it was to the Greeks, the all-sufficient unconditioned condition of all morality.[199]

A Gospel of life cannot be just a matter of rational ethics, though rational ethics is a good start; it must also be a proclamation of the vocation to divine communion which is open to all who bear the name of human, even in the womb, even when in terminal illness they cannot speak a word.

Clearly, we are not living in felicitous times, either in civil society or – up to a point – in the Church.

Yet, as if by compensation, such times are fruitful in opportunities to form the virtue of fortitude. In the muck gold can glimmer. J. R. R. Tolkien puts it well in words given to Haldir in *The Lord of the Rings*:

> The world is indeed full of peril, and in it there are many dark places; but still there is much that is fair, and though in all lands love is now mingled with grief, it grows perhaps the greater.[200]

Chapter Seven

FOR THE EROTICALLY ABSORBED: ON THE NATURE OF LUST

Introduction

This may appear to be a curious topic to include in a set of apologias. A spot of explanation seems in order. In my first ten or fifteen years in first the Religious life and then the priesthood – so, from 1970 to 1985 or thereabouts – the assumption was that sexual ethics was the point on which traditional Catholicism and cultural modernity collided most violently. Many modern Church historians would be in agreement that the fiasco surrounding *Humanae Vitae* was the beginning of the theological attempt to unravel the woollen ball of magisterial authority and to show that the line of wool, once stretched out, was neither attached very securely to its supposed origins in Christian beginnings nor firmly connected to its proper end in the docile hearing of the Word of God in Tradition as found among the Catholic faithful to whom was now ascribed the right to reject moral doctrine or at any rate an indefinite capacity to postpone the 'receiving' of its teaching. After *Humanae Vitae* came *Persona Humana* which reaffirmed the traditional vetoes to the trio of masturbation, homosexual practice, and pre-marital heterosexual intercourse, all of which had likewise been given a clean bill of emotional health by contemporary sexology. Surely some way had to be found to circumvent these prohibitions, or what a contemporary commentator on the second of these documents termed 'the atavistic thinking of a theological backwoodsman', i.e. Paul VI. Granted that the issues so far mentioned were indeed already hot potatoes in Paul's pontificate, I suppose I shouldn't have been that surprised when, ten years or so later, towards the end of the 1990s, a course of evening conferences at Blackfriars Cambridge on the seven deadly sins left me in a slightly invidious position. The series had not been my idea, but the house chapter had readily accepted it (seven being such a convenient number, since, when prefaced by an introductory lecture, as it turned out on Prudentius' moralizing poem, the *Psychomachia* or war of the vices and virtues, the resultant total of eight fitted precisely the length of a Cambridge term). It fell to me as prior to distribute the topics or rather, in the democratic manner of Dominicans, to invite the members of the Community to choose their own topic. And of course no-one chose lust. People seemed to find the talk moderately helpful. At any rate I escaped without lynching. Granted the currency of charges brought against the Catholic Church for the 'lack of realism' of her sexual ethic, I think it merits revisiting here.

My literary equipment consisted in the *Dictionnaire de théologique catholique* and a variety of sexological works from the Cambridge University Library which, I must say as a testimony to the training of the librarians, failed to raise even the suggestion of an eyebrow as I signed them out in the place of my more customary readings in German dogmatic theology. The *Dictionnaire* deals with the subject of lust in two places: first, under the ancient and mediaeval name of this vice, *luxuria*, or, in French, *luxure* (seventeen columns), and secondly, under the heading 'Spouses, duties of', where it considers what it calls 'intra-conjugal lust'(eight and a half columns, and so precisely half of what it has to say on lust in general whether in its more standard or its more spectacularly deviant manifestations). The reader is also offered further references to articles on fornication, adultery, incest, *le stupre* (that is, the deflowering of virgins), rape, and what the *Dictionnaire* terms 'carnal sacrilege', i.e. a sin of lust committed by, to or with a person specially consecrated to God as a Religious or priest. These additional essays amount to another eleven columns, and provide one with, I take it, an intelligent and representative statement of the consensual position of Catholic theology in the pontificates of the last two Popes Pius. As was usual in the moral theology of that older generation, for reasons of modesty and discretion – *la pudeur* – the authors of these articles shift from French into Latin whenever they have something especially juicy to describe. We today may be tempted to think that convention rather comic, but I hope to show it is an important witness to the true nature of well-directed sexual desire.

'Well-directed sexual desire'

Perhaps I can begin with that formulation: 'the true nature of well-directed sexual desire', which I found in what I discovered to be the best of the books I had lugged away from the library. It was by Roger Scruton, whose own spiritual odyssey has taken him at times close to the Catholic Church if he is also, as a philosopher, somewhat too Kantian to get beyond phenomenology into intrinsic validity of meaning based on the nature of creatures, the divinely caused.[201] Scruton's concept of 'well-directed sexual desire' readily gives us its opposite, the concept of 'ill-directed sexual desire', which provides us with the key to the vice of *luxuria* or lust. The *Dictionnaire* author defines lust in seemingly identical terms. It is, he writes, a disordered appetite for venereal delight, or a disordered use of such delight. Here the word 'appetite' denotes the inner motivations and aspirations which belong to our inclinations, while the word 'use' stands for inclinations that pass over into actions we carry out in the body. There is, however, as you will see as I progress, a reason why my definition and that of the *Dictionnaire* don't quite coincide: which exemplifies how my approach is that of a hermeneutic of continuity not identity or discontinuity. The distinction picks up the nuance of 'don't quite' coincide.

It is certainly true that there is something to be said in favour of defining the sin of lust in terms of a disorder in the pursuit of carnal delight. First, over against Manicheans or hyper-Puritans who find the very notion of carnal delight reprehensible, to speak of lust as a disordered appetite for or an inappropriate attainment of such delight tells us straightaway that there can be such a thing as a well-ordered appetite for the use of the reality concerned. Enjoyment of viewing or handling the body of another with an eye to coupling with that body in physical union is not an evil *per se*. Secondly, the *Dictionnaire*'s way of speaking has the advantage of maintaining contact with what (so far as one call tell) is the popular perception of the issues involved. That what the *Dictionnaire* calls 'venereal delight' should be located *in the sexual organs themselves* corresponds to a widespread conviction that sexual pleasure is essentially a physical sensation, comparable except in its context to the pleasure we experience in, for example, stepping into a warm bath. Actually, however, the word *delectatio*, 'delight', often used in preference to *voluptas*, 'pleasure', by classical Catholic moralists since at least St Thomas, has a wider connotation than simply the idea of a pleasurable sensation. As the *Dictionnaire* presents it, delight of whatever kind is the enjoyment an appetite finds in the presence or possession of its own proper good. It is the joy that some aspect of our nature as desiring beings finds in considering what fills that desire and *to that extent* fulfils our nature as a whole. Carnal delight is simply one colour in a spectrum of delightfulness set within our reach, of which the most important varieties are for the *Dictionnaire* first, the purely spiritual delight which the soul in the higher ranges of its capacity finds in its own spiritual good, and secondly, the 'sensuous spiritual delight' (in French *délectation spirituelle sensible*) which in loving God or a friend suffuses through tenderness even our bodies themselves. (The great doctors of such sensuous spiritual delight are of course St Bernard and St Aelred.)

It is, I find, precisely the humane and holistic way in which the tradition has presented delight as something wider than a pleasurable sensation which makes one hesitate in following the *Dictionnaire* when it speaks of carnal delight as essentially located in the sexual organs. Of course no one could deny that the stimulation of these organs produces pleasure, but the question is whether sexual desire (here I revert to Scruton's term) is itself just a desire for sexual pleasure, a desire which could in principle by satisfied equally well by masturbation as by courtship – or indeed, even better, if Oscar Wilde was correct when he famously commended the former of those two on the grounds that it was cleaner, more efficient, and you meet a better class of person. It seems to me that the definition of lust as a disordered pursuit of carnal delight – if, at any rate, that definition is combined with the thought that such delight is basically a localized pleasure – plays into the hands of reductionist and ultimately materialist accounts of sexuality that are incompatible with a Catholic anthropology, the Catholic Christian understanding of what it is, philosophically and theologically speaking, that human beings are.

What I mean by a reductionist and ultimately materialist account of sexuality is one where sexuality is treated simply as a bodily state common to animals and humans, a state in which certain organs in certain circumstances become irritated or aroused and require relief through a sexual act whose essential role is to discharge or release tension. That was the philosophy underlying the notorious Kinsey Report produced between the years 1948 and 1953 in the United States, a document which had a pretty disastrous influence on education and even legislation in this area. To regard the localized pleasures of the sexual act as the aim or object in desire is to ignore the fact that, unlike the animals, our delight in the fulfilling of such desire, *when it is well-directed*, concerns not only physical pleasure and not even first and foremost physical pleasure but also and principally a delight which is ours through recognizing *the meaning of the other person's gesture*. What distinguishes the sexuality of the rational animal, the 'personal animal', is that we respond not only in our body but also in our soul, to the presence or the thought of another.

Genitalia or face?

The primary disorder or misdirectedness we must identify in lust is that it fails to respect this principle by seeking in the body of another or in some simulacrum of that body – a visual image or a mental image – simply a means to the pleasurable pacification of the state of stimulus of a physical organ. That this is incorrect can be inferred from one indisputable fact which I owe to Scruton (again). When the portrayal of sexuality is not pornographically debased by concentration on the genitalia, it tends to centre on the *faces* of those who are linked by erotic love. The face has little relation to sexual powers yet it is of supreme importance in the transaction of desire. In blushing, smiling, laughing, the face doesn't function merely as a bodily part but as the expression of the whole person. The role of the face here points to the crucial truth that chaste eros involves the revelation and so the discovery of another person: in their body, of course, not out of it, and in such a way that the experience of embodiment is co-operatively heightened in the inter-action between the two persons concerned. Sexual desire that is simply transferable from one person to another because any one with roughly the right body shape will do just as well is internally defective, then, internally corrupted – which is why prostitution must be accounted a moral evil.

Many of the prohibitions issued in the name of traditional moral practice, not just in Judaeo-Christian societies but in others as well, follow from the fact that ill-directed sexual desire, namely lust, neglects the interpersonal conditions of carnal delight – delight in another through union in the body. For instance, it at once becomes clear why the sexual act or any close approach to it, belongs essentially to the private, rather than the public, sphere, and needs to take place in seclusion from the gaze of others. Where there are onlookers, third parties, the focus of arousal shifts from the embodiment of the persons to their simply having bodies, and straightaway this takes us to the idea of the obscene which is the idea of so displaying or representing the sexual act that the body, rather than the embodied person, becomes uppermost in the thoughts of those involved. Here we are already half way to the notion of bestiality: the willingness to exploit for pleasure the sexual readiness of animals.

Of course, bestiality, or even a bestial attitude towards human sexuality is a form of lustfulness of which it would be an injustice to the animal creation to say that it brings us down to their level. Only a rational being can stoop to the indignity of suffering an irrational sentiment. The animals have their own rationale for their activity. The point is that their rationale is not ours. Lust, then, is the desire for orgasm separated from an approach to another incarnate person in their uniqueness. Even before its expression in particular perversions such as obscenity or bestiality, rape or promiscuity, it is already something perverted: it is, in the vocabulary of the *Dictionnaire*, a disordered appetite, or it is, in the Scrutonian idiom, an ill-directedness of desire. When well-ordered or well-directed, sexual desire is not interested in someone's body but in the embodiment of the other. Interest in someone's body sheerly for its own sake is always something immodest, and if that someone fails to feel degraded by it their attitude is immodest likewise since it is acquiescence in their own instrumentalisation for the purposes of sexual release. That is why English law rightly criminalizes indecent exposure as a form of criminal assault.

Desire and love

Here we can move on a stage. Well-directed or rightly ordered carnal desire tends, we can say, towards love, that is, towards a sense of commitment to another founded on mutual desire. Through being overcome by the embodied presence of the other, two persons are rendered deeply vulnerable to each other and such vulnerability is only tolerable through mutual commitment. How far that mutual commitment reaches becomes clear when we consider how every developed form of well-directed sexual desire will always tend to go beyond some present encounter to a project of inner union with its object through the dedication of one person to the other – which is why the expression of desire has its rightful place in the natural covenant we call marriage. Fornication and, *a fortiori*, adultery, are for this reason essentially lustful actions.

The French Existential philosopher Jean-Paul Sartre apparently believed that authentic sexual love is impossible. Genuine, well-directed desire aims to possess the other in his or her freedom, and this is self-contradictory. It is to want to possess as an object that which can only exist as a subject. For Sartre, no-one can be possessed in their freedom. The proposal is inherently absurd. It would be trying to eat your cake (that is, to ingest or absorb the freedom of the other) while still having your cake (that is, claiming to revere the other as other). In marriage, however, two people so give themselves to each other that each one makes a vow to find his or her freedom *through* the other. The marriage vow 'until death do us part' is essential if one person is to commit themselves to find their freedom through the other by way of a timeless loyalty. This overcomes Sartre's dilemma: in principle, at any rate. It is only realistic to note, however, that when what Sartre predicts comes to pass, a dreadful cycle of frustration, oppression, and renewed frustration ensues. That is why after the Fall the natural covenant needs healing through its taking up into a sacrament where both wills, both agencies, both freedoms, submit to their common but transcendent Saviour, the God-man, with a view to becoming signs of his charity.

At that moment, the problem changes its character, since the crucial question for the flourishing of a specifically Christian marriage is the responsiveness of each partner to the grace of God. In the sacrament of marriage the natural marriage vow remains fundamental. It is the 'matter' of the sacrament. What has changed is the form, shape and framework of the union, and these change precisely in order to make new resources available through the grace of the Holy Trinity in Jesus Christ.

Married fruitfulness

Such married love, so seen, is not only constructive of the sense of self-worth as persons of those who love. It also enables each partner to do the other the more particular good of rendering him or her generative: fruitful in engendering a child or children. This is the single most important good of the many goods the partners can do for each other: to allow the other not only to be affirmed but to be creative, or as J. R. R. Tolkien might say, 'sub-creative': responsible for the existence of fresh human beings, not simply fictively, in imaginative extensions of the world, but in enduring reality, for these beings are endowed with immortal souls and capable of everlasting bliss. That is why the intention to deprive sexual congress of its naturally procreative aspect by rendering oneself deliberately infertile brings about the possibility, as the *Dictionnaire* recognizes, of lust inside marriage as well as outside it. This too changes the direction of sexual desire from the right. As Pope John Paul II expounded in his 'theology of the body', artificial contraception does not only deny the generative meaning of the marital relationship. It also undermines the unitive aspect of marital love, since it truncates the eloquence with which each partner gives themselves to the other in the language of the body.

A young man aiming at marriage whom I instructed recently as a convert presented me with a dilemma. The *Catechism of the Catholic Church* both invites people to celebrate sexual intercourse as a joy, and, by implication, to abstain from it as an ascetical practice, since as with all the laity they have a call to follow the evangelical counsels not in their letter, of course, but nevertheless in their spirit. He felt it would be more consonant with the moral teaching of the Church on contraception simply to say that, when the initial marriage relation is firmly sealed through intercourse and the work of child-bearing done, the couple should remain continent from that time on. The emphasis on the joy of sex was out of place he thought in this context. I put this point to a married graduate student of mine, also a convert, in Oxford. His response was that the *Catechism*'s words about joy were simply an attempt to explicate the older concept of the intrinsic good of sexual congress (the anti-Manichaean or anti-hyper-Puritan point I made at the outset of this chapter). How a given couple are to inter-relate the two imperatives: to affirm their delight in each other as embodied persons and to withhold themselves from affirming that delight because the Kingdom, God, is a greater and more ultimate good still, this *is* – he explained to me – the same as the question how does a non-contracepting Christian marriage work.

It is true that eventually our sexual powers wither away, and, if only when we fall into dust, all the works of Viagra are as Babylon and Tyre. It is worth remembering how the poetic imagination has sometimes expressed this eschatology, paradoxical as it may seem, in scatology. The organs which mediate the good that is the highest and most concrete fruit of sexual love, children, as well as the wider if more diffused good which both intercourse and procreation serve, the union of the partners, are also the organs of excretion. The sexual organs are situated *inter urinam et faeces*. Love, warned W. B. Yeats, 'has pitched his mansion in the house of excrement'. It can be argued that this is a providentially well-chosen arrangement. By choosing as the organs of sexual desire our most passive organs, to which we find ourselves submitting when, as we say, we 'have to answer the call of nature' by visiting the lavatory, God made it possible for us to be more thoroughly overcome by each other than would otherwise have been the case and thus to take our sexual selves seriously but not too deadly seriously.

The place of modesty

There is a delicate moral chemistry at work here, and it mandates a virtue called modesty in the matter of glances, gestures and utterances involving the sexual organs of nameable persons, including our own. Anthropologists have noted how tribal groups that go about publicly naked suffer shame when their private parts are the object of unsolicited attention. When not attending conferences about lust we rightly use circumlocutions in these matters, notably the phrase 'to make love': a good one, in that it avoids the implication that the participants are united merely as bodies in the act that unites them. Obscene literature, such as D. H. Lawrence's *Lady Chatterley's Lover* is not offensive because it portrays erotic love, but because of its prurience in observing too closely the intimacy to which an unembarrassed use of more physical words belongs.

The controversy over the book revealed how little understood, even by many Christians, sexual purity had become by the 1960s and this is an important aspect of the so-called sexual emancipation of the period, which is itself key background, as everyone agrees, to the large-scale rejection in the West of the Pauline encyclical from which I started out. In traditional societies, sexual purity was not valued because it expressed contempt for or repudiation of sexuality. On the contrary, training in chastity was seen as guaranteeing the possibility of true sexual fulfilment by ensuring that sexual desire was not detached from the person and contemplated curiously or obsessively as something simply physical but came into play only as the person is able to enter the realm of inter-subjective commitment with all its implications, including parenting.

Ideas of sexual abuse as pollution, of the child as innocent, of the virgin as sacrosanct, commonly derided by secular modernity at least until the recent paedophile scandals in the Church made it convenient to backtrack up to a point, are essential to sexual integrity, which itself is a condition of stable relations between those who love, and thus in turn is the foundation of the cheerful fecundity (not sterility supplemented by immigration) on which society depends. As G. K. Chesterton saw extremely clearly in the first third of the twentieth century, the withdrawal of the sacred from our culture, expressed in the rejection of these themes, brings with it the decline of its two most cherished institutions: the family and the home. These developments foster cynicism in the ill-intentioned and anxiety in the good. They also tend to denature erotic love and turn it into lust. The literature of lust is edifying insofar as it explores the destructiveness of such pollution in its host of forms which I end by listing for completeness's sake:

necrophilia, prefigured in intercourse with a drugged or sleeping person, which prides itself on the extinction of the interpersonal

paedophilia, which forces sexual expression on another before he or she can experience sexual desire as an inter-personal response

sado-masochism, which seeks to enslave the body of another while seeing one's own body as enslaved also

incest, which tries to build on a pre-existing inter-personal relation founded on parental love something that is incompatible with it and can only destroy it

masturbation, which bends sexual impulse away from interpersonal union and looks for gratification without the trouble of human encounter

homosexuality, which parodies the conjugal relation by omitting the dimensions of the otherness of the differently gendered partner.

'Th' expense of Spirit' (wrote Shakespeare) 'in a waste of shame/ is lust in action'. And he goes on: 'All this the world well knows, and yet none knows well/ To shun the heaven that leads men to this hell'.

Chapter Eight

FOR CRITICS OF CHRISTENDOM:
SECULARIZATION:
A CATHOLIC RESPONSE

Introduction

In a recent article in the new journal of cultural affairs *Standpoint* I argued that while secularization is far more of a challenge to Christianity in England than is Islam, nonetheless by seemingly strengthening the case for secularism the issue of Islam has moved centre-stage.[202] In this essay, as to some degree in that article, I want to add further, along the lines of the case presented in the opening chapters of a small book, *The Realm*,[203] that secularization presents an equally massive, and potentially even more disastrous, challenge to England – the cultural-political identity of that ancient nation which constitutes the southern half of the island of Britain, and which (I take it) for most readers of this book counts as 'home'. And finally, I want to pinpoint the crucial (as it seems to me) role of Catholicism in the construction of the historic English identity, and to make an appeal for the reinvigoration of the Catholic body which itself has suffered serious decline in the last decades.

A cul-de-sac: communitarianism

But before broaching the issue of secularization for its own sake, I wish to examine first, if briefly, what I regard as a cul-de-sac of criticism, namely, that response to the rise of the Islamic community in both numbers and confidence which applies to this issue the principles of the kind of social thought known as 'communitarianism'. The defining mark of communitarianism is its ascription to each faith community (or non-faith community for that matter) of that community's own version of public space. Communitarianism, it may be said, is the Ottoman Empire on a good day. It is the social-philosophical equivalent of the politics of 'multi-culturalism'. But the price to be paid for communitarianism, as for its favoured child, multi-culturalism, is – so the word 'multi-cultural' already indicates – the dis-integration of the cultural system of the nation as a whole.

As a supporter of 'birthright politics', also known as 'historical politics', I take the view that, in civil discourse, the phrase 'the community' should signify first and foremost the national community, which is the form humanity has taken historically under Providence on this particular piece of earth. Whether by birth or adoption, I have a *patria*, a native place. If I am indigenous, it is the place of my ancestors. If I am exogenous, then, like Ruth the Moabitess addressing Naomi, I say to those who are indigenous, 'where you lodge I will lodge; your people shall be my people... where you die I will die, and there will I be buried'.[204] So whether I am the one or the other, it is my hearth and home. Now the United Kingdom is itself a composite multi-national State, so the national community with which I am dealing is England. The proper response to communitarians should run: other communities within the greater whole that is England need to 'own' the overall public space of this national community, while simultaneously making their distinctive contribution.

So far as Islam is concerned, for an immigrant population with a peculiar (in the non-pejorative sense) religious and ethical system, that will take considerable energies of adaptation. While it is unwise to deflect its members from that primary task, a distinctive contribution by Muslims will mean the maintenance of whatever in their own customs and practices is noble and of good report, as others are able to acknowledge it with them.

One important criterion of those qualities – nobility, good report – has been hitherto congruence with the common law, whose name means: what is accepted in the king's (queen's) courts as legal norms all other juridical instances must respect. But the 1996 Arbitration Act renders binding the decision of an arbitration tribunal, however mounted, if both parties have agreed so to submit their dispute. *De facto* this has allowed, it now appears, the incorporation into the civil justice system of the sharia law. In terms of submission to sharia courts and acceptance of their decisions there seems reason to doubt – as with his intimate knowledge of the background Bishop

Michael Nazir-Ali has underlined – whether women (especially) are in all such cases genuinely free, fully in possession of English liberties.

I think it not impossible that some twentieth-century developments have aroused in even moderate Muslims a distaste for English law in its changing ethical index which has fuelled this desire for recourse to sharia, a desire entirely predictable among the more militant. In recent times, the effect of Parliamentary statute (and European legislation) has been to elide certain norms that were based on the good custom and proper tradition of a Christian society. The constitution of the family by the heterosexual, monogamous household, and the invulnerability of innocent human life from before birth until natural death are no longer secure at law. These are both points on which, at least in significant part, traditional Islam and Christianity concur.

Secular liberalism and its drawbacks

Legal developments incongruous with the Christian ethos would have been unthinkable in the United Kingdom without the aggressive incursion of secular liberalism. Such liberalism can only base rights discourse on the parity of each and all as they choose the way of life they prefer to follow, whether their preferences be well-founded in the objective moral order or not. We have moved into what the Canadian philosopher Charles Taylor has described as a period of romantic expressiveness on a mass scale, where the existentialism of a few influential figures in earlier twentieth-century European thought has now become, in a demotic version of itself, the maxim of so many men and women in the street. Allow me to do my own thing: meaning, to choose my own values.[205]

It is not pleasant to attack values, but sometimes it has to be done.

> Once we get the idea that there is a plurality of values and that we choose which ones will have a claim on us, we are ripe for the modern idea, first found in the works of Nietzsche, . . . that we *posit* our values – that is, that valuing is something we do and value is the result of doing it. But once we see that we posit values, we also see that we can equally 'unposit' them. They thus lose all authority for us. So, far from giving meaning to our lives, thinking of what is important to us in terms of values shows that our lives have no intrinsic meaning. As long as we think in terms of value positing rather than being gripped by shared concerns, we will not find anything that elicits our commitment . . . "No one dies for mere values".[206]

Connected herewith, surely, is the difficulty many people in our society have in finding strong reasons for living – and connected in turn with *that* is the too easy descent of our young into the miasma of drink and drugs. 'Strong reasons' for living, however, even or especially when they are appropriated with our mother's milk, or through breathing the social air around us, customarily take what may compendiously if somewhat barbarously be termed a 'culturo-politico-metaphysico-religious' form: the form of a comprehensively persuasive way of life. It is this form which is undergoing corrosion today.

The manner in which secularization is occurring in modern England – and the superbly competent Christian Institute at Wilberforce House, Newcastle-upon-Tyne, monitors the public aspect of this process on an almost weekly basis – is not, evidently, the coercive one of, for instance, the League of Militant Atheists in the Russia of the 1920s. Rather, we are dealing with a soft secularization which seeks to privatize religious aspiration, so that the public square can be cleared of all religious claims from whatever quarter. As with communitarianism, this too comes with a hefty price-tag attached.

Secular liberalism decreases the moral capital of the culture, which derives, or so I would argue, from its historic (Judaeo-Christian) patrimony which itself incorporated what was best from the ancient world. It entails the shrinking in public life of the metaphysical imagination, which becomes ever more unable to advert to the spiritual dimension of human existence. Indeed, the legal establishment of secularism – even if introduced in the name of communitarianism rather than liberalism – would amount to a declaration that agnosticism is now the religion, or anti-religion, of the State.

The human poverty of secular liberalism can already be inferred from the results of contemporary secularization. In modern England moral discourse is in danger of becoming a parody of infantile egoism. The moral life becomes a matter of wishes, preferences, needs and desires. It is true that the moral life begins with desire. But such desire, as Plato argued and the English historian of ancient philosophy John Rist has emphasized in his study *Real Ethics*,[207] is not the desire which leads us to pursue 'enlightened' self-interest, in the form of the hedonistic calculus which asks how I can maximize pleasure. The desire which impels the moral life is, rather, desire for the good because it is beautiful. To dignify with the term 'ethical' the expression of preference by reference to wants contravenes this principle. In terms of moral aesthetics it is ugly. That can be seen in the way typically secular liberal ethicists find it difficult to avoid the justification of moral pathologies: for example, the choices of those who freely contract to inflict physical pain on each other for the purposes of sadistic satisfaction. Outside the purview of abnormal emotionality, the combination of secularism with utilitarianism is capable of producing equally repellent effects, as in the 2008 proposal of the influential moral philosopher Baroness Warnock that elderly people in mental decline are wasting other people's lives and should be encouraged to consider it their duty to opt for euthanasia. The awareness that the good is truly beautiful such that it is fine to serve it, regardless of inconvenience – what the Hellenes termed *kalokagathia* – sits as uncomfortably with Lady Warnock's asseverations as, by contrast, it fits like a glove the moral beauty of the Church's saints, in whose lives the voices of creation in pagan antiquity entered into concert, so to say, with the biblical revelation. Pope Benedict XVI has called the saints the demonstration of Christian claims in an empirical age since between them the saints span all the main sectors of human living, from public service through education and health care to the arts and domesticity, and in those realms give evidence of a great range of virtues.

The exemplars we have in this island from the Christian past and present – and those who today, without personal faith, show in decency of life the *effects* of the Christian faith in an inherited ethos – constitute a spiritual commonwealth that is our most precious form of national wealth. In terms of real function that commonwealth is the most important part of the body politic since it shows us the *telos* or goal at which life lived in the light of a common good aims. Nothing can compare in culture-creating power with the example of people who embody the highest goods in their due order of significance.

Some people will commend a secular State simply as a pragmatic response to cultural diversity, albeit an important piece of pragmatism since it holds out the hope of social peace. They fail to see how every such response carries its own ideological load which may include substantial negatives. Considered as a State ideology, secular liberalism, paradoxically enough, has one attribute in common with the Islamist militancy that is propelling it towards power and prospective hegemony. It will not address questions of the common good in a way that can build up a firm texture for the social fabric. While Islamist terrorism seeks the outright dissolution of that texture, such liberalism merely allows it to unravel, but the result may be much the same: an atomism that destroys effective solidarity.

Atomism can be a word for separating individuals who are contemporary with one another in space. But in this social application it can also denote the dissolution of inter-human bonds across time. Secular liberalism cannot help looking for a *politics without memory*, which is why it allies so readily with mass-media pundits bound to the instant contemporaneity captured in the sound-bite. It is a modernism insouciant of the past. But, as with the *homo sovieticus* of the Bolshevik experience, its attempt to sever the past from the future produces an attitude to human living which devalues the real present, depriving it of richness of reference. The theorists of secular liberalism have their own (contractarian) 'tradition' – the late American political philosopher John Rawls is the final outworking of this, yet their tradition is not one of life, but of thought-experiments by ratiocination. It is a 'tradition' defined by enquiry into what any rational agent would do to acquire minimum security. Such theory is always inclined to deny history and particularity, including those of a religion. This does not sit well with our culture which, as the Labour Member of Parliament Denis McShane has written, 'from Shakespeare to Pope to Brontë to Orwell has been about a deeply felt sense of language and history'.[208]

More profoundly still, philosophical liberals rarely

understand the foundational character of metaphysical and religious belief and thought, which turn on how human beings are made with a deep inclination to seek and worship almighty God. Philosophical liberalism marries readily with secularism. Secularism wants to suppress the public relevance of the human orientation to transcendence, while philosophical liberalism has already lost the sense of it. By 'transcendence' here is meant a goal lying beyond humanism. Unfortunately, there is more than one way to transcend humanism. The divine way of salvation in the triune God – such is the message of the Judaeo-Christian Scriptures – goes beyond humanism by gathering in all authentic human good beyond the deaths of persons, cultures, and even the cosmos itself. This is not a counter-humanism so much as an eschatological humanism that licenses sacrifice and renunciation now. Many twenty-first-century secular liberals, still fighting High Victorian battles, do not sufficiently appreciate that the real enemies of humanism are situated a million intellectual miles from the Church, on the far boundaries of scientific technology and naturalistic ethics.

Thus, for example, scientists intrigued by 'transhumanism' are investigating, at any rate theoretically, the possibility that nano-technology and atomic re-arrangement may permit the spring-boarding of the development of a post-human species. For other transhumanists, since the world's only underlying feature is information – which itself is fluid, reconfigurable in indefinitely many ways – it should be possible to 'upload' the brain patterns of individuals, transferring them to computers, whether with prosthetic bodies attached to replace our out-of-date hardware, or simply for the purposes of continued existence in cyberspace. Meanwhile, the more radical deep ecologists castigate the human race as a vermin species afflicting Gaia, and yearn for a global pandemic as a cure, while the bioethics movement grows increasingly utilitarian, denying human beings intrinsic worth in order to justify not only abortion but eugenic infanticide.

Where, we may ask, is the dignity of the *humanum* here? Without a theological basis in the doctrine of the imagehood of God in man, such dignity is insecurely placed. It is not surprising that rational humanists have been hard put to find a stable philosophical foundation for human rights claims. Yet they need to meet the objections to the well-foundedness of those claims, objections summed up in Jeremy Bentham's dismissive description: 'nonsense on stilts'.[209]

If rational humanists struggling to defend human dignity while denying man's creation in the divine image may be said to mistake the foundations of anthropology, secularists, through using the legislature to press human rights claims in new directions, may be said to misunderstand the nature of the State. Where its higher functions are concerned, over and above the defence of the national territory and the preservation of fundamental order (including, as we have seen recently, economic order), it is not the task of the State to invent new moralities, but to *guard the spiritual civilization of its own society*. For the legislature and judiciary that means being guided in the formulation and interpretation of laws by the moral ethos which forms a given society's spiritual patrimony. For the executive it means self-restraint, since the urge to intervene at as many points as possible in civil society, whether administratively or by proposing new laws, undermines the will of citizens to collaborate with each other in community-building projects at all levels of life. Where charities and other voluntary associations are so managed by State action that they become little more than expressions of a government project, the result will eventually be for civil society to wither away.

Recent legislation obliging Catholic adoption agencies to place children with civilly partnered foster-parents of the same sex offended on both counts – respect for the historic moral ethos and the need to leave civil society its proper space. On this issue Catholic spokesmen were accused of seeking to gain for the Church a special exemption – which could all too easily be compared with the wish of some Muslims for the full recognition of sharia law. In a sense the critics were – after a Pickwickian fashion – right. Catholics were concerned for consistency of religious practice in their own Communion, as no doubt zealous Muslims are for the coherence of the *umma*. But because the reaction of the Church was to a signal transgression of a prime principle of a spiritual civilization formed by the historic Christianity of the English people, the Church was also protesting in the name of the historic moral ethos of this nation, which politicians should respect, if not indeed serve. In another sense the critics were altogether wrong, since in a complementary perspective the Church's opposition was entirely without self-regard. Catholics objected to the inflation of State power vis-à-vis civil society, with its attendant threat to other groups – and, for that matter, individuals – seeking to pursue charitable ends which could only benefit the social whole. As Benedict XVI remarked in his first encyclical *Deus caritas est:*

> We do not need a State which regulates and controls everything, but a State which, in accordance with the principle of subsidiarity, generously acknowledges and supports initiatives arising from the different social forces and combines spontaneity with closeness to those in need.[210]

As English Christians we also want to live in a public order that will make it easy, not difficult, to transmit what I have called the culturo-politico-metaphysico-religious form of the good life to our children and grandchildren.

I have been describing some of the drawbacks to a secularizing State which, in one perspective, is chiefly a device to ease life for the non-religious. That reminds us how secularization, though it may in part be unintended, arrived at serendipitously – as suggested by analysts as different as Taylor, already mentioned, and John Milbank of the University of Nottingham – is not an inevitable process. As fully achieved in societies where religion has been successfully marginalised, secularization is the work of elites who want to free themselves and the world they inhabit from any appeal to an authority that invokes transcendence.[211] The so-called 'Whig Grand Narrative', for which the progressive emancipation of mankind, prepared by Renaissance and Reformation, comes about through the birth of modern science and the emergence of the secular State, is far from incontestable, even if we balk at the American historian who has called it 'not much more than paid political advertisements for English liberalism'.[212] That remark, by raising the question of the distinctive character of the English tradition, has at least the advantage of enabling me to pass more or less smoothly to the next stage of my exposition, which I entitle:

A privileged moment: the debate over English identity

The debate over English identity, itself spurred by a combination of elements – internal devolution in the United Kingdom, reflection on the wider implications of membership of the European Union, the scale of recent immigration, and the breakdown of corporate memory facilitated by a range of factors, from media absorption in the contemporary to the deficiencies of history teaching in schools – constitutes, I believe, a privileged moment for English Christianity. It provides a forum in which one can put forward the case that the Judaeo-Christian tradition furnishes what is most foundationally form-giving in English society and culture, while simultaneously allowing that, on grounds of conscience, there are individuals and groups who cannot make that tradition fully their own. As always, freedom of conscience can and should be balanced against the interests of a particular historical society as a whole.

A nation, like a civilization, needs a shared vision of reality, at any rate in fair degree. It is unclear that a great civilization can be formed except on the ground of metaphysical or religious principle. The historian Christopher Dawson predicted in the closing years of the Second World War the eventual death of any civilization that loses hold on its own religious basis.[213] There is no other obvious way in which to secure the foundations of ethics, or to inspire a high artistic culture, or to animate institutions which will be seedbeds of the virtues. In the case of England, whose emergence as a nation coincides with its conversion, this can only be Christianity, with its Judaic background, and more especially the 'New Israel' of the Catholic Church.

Every people needs a narrative. The ethicist Alasdair MacIntyre has registered his anxiety that, in a liberal society of ahistorical outlook, the individual will prove unable to form a firm identity, as member of some shared story, or to acquire clear criteria for the definition of a shared good.[214] In a national community, not to be able to situate oneself as a bearer of a shared narrative is bad for mental and moral health. Such a community should help me to answer the question, 'Who am I?', even if my eventual answer entails some criticism of that story and even a degree of detachment from it. Along with the formation of identity goes, so MacIntyre has it, the acquiring of criteria for defining a shared good, for some range of non-arbitrary values I can cherish. We can commend Catholic Christianity to our fellow-countrymen not least on this basis.

The thousand years of Catholic Christianity which preceded the Reformation settlement are responsible for the origins of the English literary imagination, for the principles of the common law, for the concept of a covenanted people under God which permeates the induction of the sovereign, and for the range of virtues which have been commended, and sometimes practised, in English society and culture. In the context of a more-than-national Church this entailed a measured trans-nationalism. When the mediaeval idea of Christendom weakened, the early modern nation-state tried more vigorously to instrumentalise the Church, politicising the divine rather than – by exposure to a transcendent Good – divinising the *polis*.[215] This was the Machiavellianism of the Cecils and the first Elizabeth, which has taken in so many English patriots of the *Westward Ho!* school of thinking.

Recent historiography, however, has pushed back the origins of English identity and State formation well behind the Reformation, with which Victorian apologists for Protestantism were too ready to identify them, and for that matter behind the Norman Conquest too. Englishness is a very ancient thing.[216] Such historians of the Anglo-Saxon period as James Campbell and the late Patrick Wormald have spoken of the 'wide extent of "emotional and ideological commitment"' to the later Anglo-Saxon State which achieved by dynastic means a political union for all England in 927. Within this dynastic context, the two most crucial factors in play were law and religion. For Wormald, there was already by that date 'a remarkably precocious sense of common "Englishness"' defined, for the literate by Bede.[217] By contrast, the Reformation, especially but not exclusively in its Calvinist dimension, can be seen as an attempt to internationalise England in a cosmopolis of the Reformed – over against the doctrinal consciousness rendered native by hundreds of years of mental accustoming which found expression in traditional liturgies, devotions of varied lineage and date, iconography (including the new printed images), and a host of customs and practices too many to enumerate though wonderfully evoked in studies by Eamon Duffy. Writing of recent historians of the Tudor age, Jonathan Clark, probably the premier living historian of the transition between early modern and modern England, reports that

> the few Anglicans who are historically aware now often depict the Church of England as essentially a radical Protestant denomination with a revolutionary foundation in the early sixteenth century . . .[218]

such that, in the absence of some more coherent narrative of the *longue durée* that might confer a greater moral authority, the Anglican Church has no real option at the present time other than to follow the direction of a free-floating public opinion, for example in the matter of feminism and the gay issue. Even though the memory of the pre-Reformation past sparks catholicising movements in Anglicanism every half century or so, this judgment, itself offered by a practising member of the Church of England, ought to be taken with full seriousness. It is at any rate a clear response to the questions about Anglican identity put so sharply by Cardinal Walter Kasper at the 2008 Lambeth Conference.

The role of English Catholicism

In historical perspective the establishment of the Church of England at law is far from rendering superfluous, then, the public role of the English Catholic Church. But any plausible occupancy of that role has as its precondition the future institutional flourishing of the English Catholic Church. Yet this is not a future which from every angle looks too rosy at present.

Here the strategy I advocate is one which might be called 'in depth re-confessionalisation'. In this slogan, the adverbial phrase – 'in depth' – and the noun – 're-confessionalisation' – should be given equal weight. 'Re-confessionalisation' speaks of the renaissance of a kind of Catholicism that would be more secure in its own identity, both doctrinal and cultural, than has been the case in recent decades, where milk has been spilt in the name of ecumenical adjustment and accommodation to the social life-ways of others. That more secure identity is needed, not least, in order the better to counter the force of secularism. With too diluted an ecclesial glue, hearts, minds, sensibilities do not bond.

By contrast, the adverbial phrase 'in depth' indicates that re-confessionalisation does not mean a sectarian Catholic tribalism which in any case would be incapable of taking responsibility for England's soul, nor does it involve an attempt to recreate the Church of the 1950s, which, though its unity and confidence were exemplary, showed its Achilles' heel by the manner in which its adherents subsequently fell away. A deep Catholicism, as portrayed in the book of that name by the French theologian Henri de Lubac, is not simply sure of its dogmatic basis and at home in its corporate memory, though these are essential.[219] It is also profoundly rooted in the Scriptures, the Fathers, the great doctors and spiritual teachers, and receptive to whatever is lovely in the human world of any and every time and place, which the Word draws to himself by assuming human nature into union with his own divine person.

When I think of the internal renewal of the Catholic Church in England the kind of things that come to mind are the rediscovery of Catholic Christianity as an adventure in ideas through the claims of Christian philosophy and the diffusion of a rich dogmatic vision through much-improved catechesis; a re-enchanting of the Liturgy which is our primary induction into the nature of prayer and so the mystical; a re-focussing of Catholic institutions, from family, through school, to health-care agencies, on an approach to life that is informed by the intellectual and mystical facets of revelation, so that people are gripped, and discover what I earlier called not simply values but 'strong reasons for living' through their participation in these shared concerns.

The witness of the Church to the human good, over against the more crabbed and confined, or fragile and evanescent, version of that good found in secularism (and in this chapter I have mainly been concerned to point up that contrast), needs to be accompanied by her popular revival as a public force.

Conclusion

The late Maurice Cowling, in the foreword to the third and last volume of his *Religion and Public Doctrine in Modern England*, asked whether, after the 'doubt and turmoil of the 60s and 70s', the Catholic priesthood in England, any more than its Anglican or Nonconformist counterparts, has what he termed the 'requisite normality, serenity and self-confidence to address the Christianity which is latent in English life'.[220] 'Criticising the critics', by establishing appropriate apologias for Catholic Christianity today, is integral to restoring that serene confidence. I hope this collection of such apologias can be useful in this regard in some small way.

NOTES

[1] *Pascendi*, 1.

[2] Ibid., 2.

[3] Ibid., 5.

[4] Ibid., 6.

[5] 'Intellectualism' was Tyrrell's name for the (in his view, misplaced) concern of Scholasticism to supply for revelation a conceptual grid enabling its systematic expression in doctrinal theology. A clear expression of his view is the essay 'The Relation of Theology to Devotion', originally published in *The Month* 94 (November, 1899), pp. 461-473, and reprinted in idem, *Through Scylla and Charybdis, or, The Old Theology and the New* (London, Longmans, Green, and Co., 1907), pp. 85-105.

[6] See for an account of Blondel's case in *L'Action*, A. Nichols, O.P., *From Hermes to Benedict XVI. Faith and Reason in Modern Catholic Thought* (Leominster, Gracewing, 2008), pp. 157-163.

[7] *Pascendi*, 7.

[8] For a characterisation of this figure, see A. R. Vidler, *A Variety of Catholic Modernists* (Cambridge, Cambridge University Press, 1970), pp. 20-62.

[9] *Pascendi*, 30.

[10] F. von Hügel, 'John, Gospel of St', *Encyclopaedia Brittanica* (11th edition, Cambridge, Cambridge University Press, 1910), XV, pp. 452-458. For the timing, see M. de la Bedoyère, *The Life of Baron von Hügel* (London, Dent, 1951), pp. 190-191.

[11] *Pascendi*, 33.

[12] Ibid., 35.

[13] Ibid., 37.

[14] Ibid.

[15] We should note, however, that Blondel claimed never to have raised the *theological* question of the necessity of the supernatural, only the philosophical one of how the option for the supernatural must be considered if it presents itself. See again A. Nichols, O.P., *From Hermes to Benedict XVI*, op. cit., pp. 168-169.

[16] *Pascendi*, 41.

[17] Ibid., 42.

[18] Ibid., 45.

[19] Ibid., 55.

[20] H. Bürkle, A. Görres, W. Kasper (eds), *Tiefenpsychologische Deutung des Glaubens? Anfragen an Eugen Drewermann* (Freiburg, Herder, 1988).

[21] This prolific author has provoked a correspondingly copious literature in Germany: thus A. Sobel, *Eugen-Drewermann-Bibliographie: Primär- und Sekundärliteratur, Rezensionenverzeichnis, Bibliographie zum Fall Drewermann, Einführung* (Wiesbaden, Verlag A. Sobel, 1992).

[22] Centre Jean Bart, *De quel Dieu les sacrements sont signe?* (n.p., 1975), p. 15, cited R. Amerio, *Iota Unum. A Study of Changes in the Catholic Church in the Twentieth Century* (English translation, Kansas City, Sarto House, 1996), p. 118.

[23] M. J. Wrenn, *Catechisms and Controversies. Religious Education in the Postconciliar Years* (San Francisco, Ignatius, 1991); idem, with K. D. Whitehead, *Flawed Expectations. The Reception of the 'Catechism of the Catholic Church'* (San Francisco, Ignatius, 1996).

[24] L. T. Johnson (with W. S. Kurz), *The Future of Catholic Biblical Scholarship. A Constructive Conversation* (Grand Rapids, Eerdmans, 2002).

[25] Idem, *The Real Jesus. The Misguided Quest for the Historical Jesus and the Truth of the Traditional Gospels* (San Francisco, Harper, 1996).

[26] Cited in J. Pearce, *Old Thunder. A Life of Hilaire Belloc* (London, Harper Collins, 2002), p. 164.

[27] *Jesus Christ the Bearer of the Water of Life*, 1. 3.

[28] H. U. von Balthasar, *The Scandal of the Incarnation. Irenaeus against the Heresies* (English translation, San Francisco, Ignatius, 1990).

[29] Idem, 'Irenaeus' in *The Glory of the Lord. A Theological Aesthetics. Volume 2. Studies in Theological Styles: Clerical Styles* (English translation, T. and T. Clark, Edinburgh and San Francisco 1984), pp. 31-94.

[30] K. Mongrain, *The Systematic Thought of Hans Urs von Balthasar. An Irenaean Retrieval* (New York , Continuum, 2002).

[31] *Dominus Jesus*, 2.

[32] *Nostra aetate*, 2, cited ibid.

[33] *Dominus Jesus*, 3.

[34] Ibid., 4.

[35] I say 'in some form' owing to a hesitation about the second, the distinction between faith and belief. Irenaeus contrasts biblical faith with Gnostic claims to saving *knowledge* of self. Nor did the Gnostics accept that pagan religions attained the truth about God. However, in *Adversus haereses* II. 14. 9, Irenaeus complains that the Gnostics sought to gain credibility among pagans by using for the Aeons names already in circulation for the Hellenistic deities, and insinuating that such deities were (ontological) images of the Aeons.

[36] Irenaeus, *Adversus haereses* III. 3. 1.

[37] H. Bettenson (ed.), *Documents of the Christian Church* (London, Oxford University Press, 1943; 1956), p. 97.

[38] *Dominus Jesus*, 4.

[39] Ibid.

[40] In one sense, Gnosticism is a Christian heresy, a point stressed by E. Yamauchi, *Pre-Christian Gnosticism: A Survey of the Proposed Evidences* (Grand Rapids, Eerdmans,1983), and

S. Petrément, *Le Dieu séparé: Les origins du Gnosticisme* (Paris, Cerf, 1984). In another sense it develops from an ambient sensibility which preceded it: thus B. A. Pearson, 'Jewish Elements in Gnosticism and the Development of Gnostic Self-Definition', in E. P. Sanders (ed.), *Jewish and Christian Self-Definition, 1: The Shaping of Christianity in the Second and Third Centuries* (Philadelphia, Fortress, 1980), pp. 151-160, and idem, 'Early Christianity and Gnosticism: A Review Essay', *Religious Studies Review* 13 (1987), pp. 1-8.

[41] *Dominus Jesus*, 6.

[42] Ibid., 7.

[43] Romans 16: 26; cf. Romans 1: 5; II Corinthians 10: 5-6.

[44] *Dominus Jesus*, 7.

[45] Ibid., 10. The best known representative of this position is probably the recently deceased Belgian Jesuit Jacques Dupuis, whose book, *Vers une théologie chrétienne du Pluralisme religieux* (Paris, Cerf, 1997) was the object of a critical 'notification' by the Holy Office in 2001. For the 'Notification' see, conveniently, the slightly abridged version 'How to Read Jacques Dupuis. The Verdict of the CDF', in the London *Tablet* for 3 March 2001.

[46] *Dominus Jesus*, 10.

[47] Irenaeus, *Adversus haereses* IV. 20. 6. See J. Ochagavía, *Visibile Patris Filius. A Study of Irenaeus's Teaching on Revelation and Tradition* (Rome, Pontificio Istituto Orientale, 1964, = *Orientalia Christiana Analecta* 171), pp. 93-94.

[48] J. Daniélou, *A History of Christian Doctrine before the Council of Nicaea. Volume 2: Gospel Message and Hellenistic Culture* (English translation, London, Darton, Longman and Todd, 1973), p. 168.

[49] Irenaeus, *Adversus haereses* IV. 20. 1.

[50] Irenaeus, *Adversus haereses* IV. 20. 5.

[51] Justin, *Second Apology* 8, 1-2; 10, 1-3; 13, 3-6; John Paul II,

Redemptoris missio 28.

[52] *Dominus Jesus*, 13.

[53] Specifically vis-à-vis his Gnostic opponents, Irenaeus complains that they 'did not understand the economy of God but had instead a multiplicity of economies – one of the Pleroma, one of the Savior, one of the Demiurge, one of the Christ, one of creation and one of the redemption.' Irenaeus turned upside down the Gnostic formula 'the economy of the Pleroma', and produced his own Christianised version 'the fulfilling of the dispensation' so as to emphasise the all-encompassing unity of an economy where, thanks to Jesus Christ the Recapitulator, all things are summed up in the Word made flesh. Thus T. L. Tiessen, *Irenaeus on the Salvation of the Unevangelized* (Metuchen, NJ, Scarecrow Press, 1993), p. 119, and cf. Irenaeus, *Adversus haereses* III. 12. 12.

[54] Cf. *Dominus Jesus*, 15.

[55] T. L. Tiessen, *Irenaeus on the Salvation of the Unevangelized*, op. cit., p. 131.

[56] *Dominus Jesus*, 16.

[57] P. Heelas, *The New Age Movement. The Celebration of Self and the Sacralization of Modernity* (Oxford, Blackwell, 1997), p. 173, cited *Jesus Christ the Bearer of the Water of Life*, 2. 4.

[58] P. Perkins, *The Gnostic Dialogue: The Early Church and the Crisis of Gnosticism* (New York, Paulist, 1980), p. 10. Perkins writes in two sentences that precede this citation: '[The Gnostics'] stratified system of salvation negated all those who were not ontologically *pneumatic*, and within the particular Gnostic individual movements, internal schisms dictated new direction rather than an authoritative institutional structure. Given all these characteristics the experience of *gnosis* is by definition anti-institution'.

[59] *Lumen gentium,* 8.

[60] *Dominus Jesus,* 16, citing *Lumen gentium,* 8.

[61] *Mysterium Ecclesiae*, 1, cited in *Dominus Jesus*, 17.

[62] *Dominus Jesus*, 18.

[63] Ibid., 19.

[64] T. L. Tiessen, *Irenaeus on the Salvation of the Unevangelized*, op. cit., p. 211.

[65] *Dominus Jesus*, 20.

[66] My part-paraphrase of *Dominus Jesus*, 20 in its use of *Redemptoris missio*, 9. A recent theological attempt to set out a case along these lines is B.-D. de la Soujeole, 'Foi implicite et religions non-chrétiennes', *Revue Thomiste* CVI, 1-2 (2006), pp. 315-334.

[67] Irenaeus, *Adversus haereses* II. 24. 1; Cyprian, *De catholicae ecclesiae unitate*, 6.

[68] L. S. Thornton, *Revelation and the Modern World, Being the First Part of a Treatise on the Form of the Servant* (Westminster, Dacre Press, 1950), p. 28.

[69] For Dreyfus' critique, see A. Nichols, O.P., 'François Dreyfus on Scripture read in Tradition', in idem, *Scribe of the Kingdom: Essays on Theology and Culture* (London, Sheed and Ward, 1994), pp. 32-77.

[70] *The Divine Office. The Liturgy of the Hours according to the Roman Rite* III (London, Collins, 1974), pp. 63*-64*.

[71] D. Fárkasfalvy, 'A Heritage in Search of Heirs: the Future of Ancient Christian Exegesis', *Communio* 25. 3 (1998), pp. 505-519, and here at p. 511.

[72] Ibid.

[73] Ibid., p. 512.

[74] Ibid.

[75] Ibid., pp. 512-513.

[76] I. de la Potterie, 'Reading Holy Scripture "in the Spirit": Is the patristic way of reading the Bible still possible today?', *Communio* 4.4 (1986), pp. 308-325, and here at p. 316.

[77] Ibid.

[78] Ibid., p. 317.

[79] Ibid., p. 318, citing M. Eliade, *Images and Symbols: Studies in Religious Symbolism*, trans. P. Mairet (New York, Sheed and Ward, 1961), p. 170.

[80] *Dei Verbum* 2.

[81] I. de la Potterie, 'Reading Holy Scripture "in the Spirit": Is the patristic way of reading the Bible still possible today?', p. 322.

[82] Ibid., pp. 322-323.

[83] Ibid., p. 323.

[84] Ibid., pp. 323-324.

[85] John 16: 13.

[86] M.-J. Lagrange, O.P., *Evangile selon saint Luc* (Paris, Gabalda, 1948, 8th edition), p. II.

[87] Letter of 26 April 1950 from Hugues Vincent, O.P., to Bruno de Solages, in H. de Lubac, S.J., *Scripture in the Tradition*, trans. L. O'Neill (New York, Herder and Herder, 2000), p. 232.

[88] Ibid.

[89] Letter of 21 June 1950 from Hugues Vincent, O.P., to Henri de Lubac, S.J., in ibid., p. 234.

[90] H. de Lubac, S.J., *Catholicism. Christ and the Common Destiny of Man*, trans. L. C. Sheppard (London, Burns and Oates, 1962), p. 91.

[91] I. de la Potterie (ed.), *L'Exégèse chrétienne aujourd'hui* (Paris, Fayard, 2000).

[92] J. Ratzinger/Benedict XVI, *Jesus von Nazareth I. Von der Taufe im Jordan bis zur Verklärung* (Herder, Freiburg, 2007), p. 15.

[93] M. Bockmuehl, 'Reason, Wisdom and the Implied Disciple of Scripture', in D. F. Ford and G. Stanton (eds), *Reading Texts, Seeking Wisdom. Scripture and Theology* (London, SCM, 2003), pp. 53-68, and here at p. 53.

[94] Ibid., pp. 53-54.

[95] Ibid., p. 54.

[96] Ibid., p. 58.

[97] Ibid., p. 59. Bockmuehl is commenting on R. D. Williams, 'The Literal Sense of Scripture', *Modern Theology* 7 (1991), pp. 121-134, reflected in idem, *On Christian Theology* (Oxford, Blackwell, 2000), pp. 44-59.

[98] M. Bockmuehl, 'Reason, Wisdom and the Implied Disciple of Scripture', art. cit., p. 63.

[99] Ibid., p. 68.

[100] Augustine, *De doctrina christiana* 4. 12.

[101] Thomas, 'The Inaugural Sermons (1256). Commendation of and Division of Sacred Scripture', in R. McInerny (ed.), *Thomas Aquinas. Selected Writings* (London, Penguin, 1998), pp. 5-12, and here at p. 12.

[102] II Timothy 3: 16.

[103] *Message to the People of God*, 3.

[104] Ibid.

[105] Ibid.

[106] Ibid., 5.

[107] Ibid.

[108] Ibid., 6.

[109] Ibid.

[110] Ibid.

[111] Benedict XVI, *Deus caritas est*, 1.

[112] *Message to the People of God*, 15.

[113] Witness A. Hunt, *The Trinity and the Paschal Mystery. A Development in Recent Catholic Theology* (Collegeville, MN, Liturgical Press, 1997), p. viii, and passim.

[114] Deuteronomy 32: 6.

[115] T. F. Torrance, *The Trinitarian Faith. The Evangelical Theology of the Ancient Catholic Church* (Edinburgh, T. and T. Clark, 1988), p. 56.

[116] Athanasius, *On the Decrees*, 15.

[117] A. Nichols, O.P., *Holy Order. The Apostolic Ministry from the*

New Testament to the Second Vatican Council (Dublin, Veritas, 1990), pp. 149-150.

[118] E.g. Starhawk, *The Spiral Dance: A Rebirth of the Ancient Religion of the Great Goddess* (San Francisco, Harper and Row, 1979), p. 8, cited B. Ashley, O.P., *Justice in the Church. Gender and Participation* (Washington, Catholic University of America Press, 1996), p. 108.

[119] C. Walker Bynum, *Fragmentation and Redemption. Essays on Gender and the Human Body in Medieval Religion* (New York, Zone Books, 1992), p. 59.

[120] T. F. Torrance, *The Trinitarian Faith,* op. cit., pp. 138-139.

[121] Irenaeus, *Adversus Haereses,* III. 11, 2.

[122] Athanasius, *Contra Arianos,* I. 47.

[123] T. F. Torrance, *The Trinitarian Faith,* op. cit., p. 191.

[124] G. Lafont, O.S.B., *God, Time and Being* (English translation, Petersham, MA, St Bede's Publications, 1992), p. 169.

[125] Hugh of Saint-Victor, *De sacramentis* I. 8. 12.

[126] Ibid., I. 10. 6-8.

[127] Ibid., I. 11-12.

[128] A good summary of Hugh's thought in this regard can be found in P. Grelot, *Sens chrétien de l'Ancien Testament. Esquisse d'un traité dogmatique* (Tournai, Desclée, 1962), pp. 54-57.

[129] Thomas Aquinas, *Summa theologiae* Ia. IIae., qq. 98-108. Strictly speaking, the treatise ends at q. 105, but qq. 106-108 are needed to show how Thomas understands the New Law in relation to the Old.

[130] M.-D. Chenu, O.P., 'La théologie de la Loi ancienne selon saint Thomas', *Revue thomiste* 51 (1961), pp. 485-497.

[131] For a nuanced discussion of Old Testament priesthood, see J. M. Scholer, *Proleptic Priests: Priesthood in the Epistle to the Hebrews* (Sheffield, JSOT, 1991), pp. 13-23. I owe this reference to the Revd Dr Merryl Blair.

[132] Genesis 14: 18-20.

[133] I Chronicles 6: 8; 24: 3.

[134] I Kings 1: 38-40.

[135] Ezekiel 40:46.

[136] II Timothy 3: 16.

[137] Cited J. Galy, *Le Sacrifice dans l'Ecole française* (Paris, Nouvelles Editions latines, 1951), p. 301.

[138] For some indications of relevant texts, see A. Vanhoye, *Old Testament Priests and the New Priest according to the New Testament* (English translation, Petersham, MA, St Bede's Publications, 1986), pp. 44-47.

[139] 11Q13.

[140] But one can note that texts from the Canon speak of divine guarantees for the continuing salvific relevance of the priestly institutions: e.g. Sirach 45: 7 on the 'eternal covenant' given to the Aaronic priesthood; Jeremiah 33: 17-18 on how, in parallel with the irreversibility of the promise to David of a line of sons on the royal throne, so the Levitical priesthood will never lack successors to offer sacrifice; Malachi 3: 3-4 on the purification of the sons of Levi on the Day of the Lord so that they shall be able to offer right offerings. The crucial role of the 'sons of Zadok' in the restored eschatological Temple of Ezekiel has already been mentioned.

[141] Mark 1: 24.

[142] John 6: 69.

[143] Leviticus 21:6; II Chronicles 23: 6; 35: 3.

[144] Exodus 28: 36.

[145] G. Friedrich, 'Beobachtungen zur messianischen Hohe-priesterwartung bei den Synoptikern', *Zeitschrift für Theologie und Kirche* 53 (1956), pp. 265-311.

[146] 'Haec pontifex summus, propitiator ipse et propitiatorium, sacerdos et sacrificium, pro nobis oravit': thus Rupert of Deutz, *In Evangelium S. Joannis Commentatorium libri XIV* , at *Patrologia Latina* 169, 764B.

[147] John 1: 1-15.

[148] A. Feuillet, *The Priesthood of Christ and his Ministers* (English translation, Garden City, NY, Doubleday), op. cit., p. 25.

[149] Exodus 24.

[150] Leviticus 16.

[151] Matthew 26: 28.

[152] A. Charbel, *Zebah selamin. Il sacrificio pacifico* (Jerusalem, Studium Biblicum Franciscanum, 1967), p. 84. But it has been pointed out that for the Targums all sacrifice is expiatory: thus M. McNamara, M.S.C., *Targum and Testament. Aramaic Paraphrases of the Hebrew Bible: A Light on the New Testament* (Shannon, Irish University Press, 1972), p. 129. To what extent chronology allows the Targums to be used to throw light on the New Testament is, however, something of a disputed question.

[153] M. Barker, *The Gate of Heaven. The History and Symbolism of the Temple in Jerusalem* (London, SPCK, 1991), op. cit., p. 62. Margaret Barker's work has to be used with caution, since she seems to consider the Old Testament Canon wrongly drawn up, but she is acutely sensitive to the cultic and mysteric aspects of Israel's faith, and I shall draw on her scholarship without, however, total commitment to her theses either in detail or as a whole.

[154] Isaiah 52: 11 – 53: 12.

[155] P. Grelot, *Le ministère de la nouvelle Alliance* (Paris, Cerf, 1967), p. 44, with an internal citation of Isaiah 53: 12.

[156] And as Aage Bentzen puts it, 'We can state historically that Jesus of Nazareth must have considered Isaiah 53 the programme of His life', *King and Messiah* (English translation, Oxford 1970, 2nd edition), p. 48.

[157] Ephesians 5: 2.

[158] John 17: 19. See on this A. Feuillet, *The Priesthood of Christ and his Ministers*, op. cit., p. 35.

[159] Matthew 27: 51; Mark 15: 38; Luke 23: 45.

[160] M. Barker, *The Gate of Heaven*, op. cit., p. 124.

[161] See Exodus 36: 35, 37 for the veil; Exodus 39: 8, 24, 29, for the vestments.

[162] Philo, *Questions on Exodus* II. 85; Josephus, *Jewish Wars* V. 212-213: these references are taken from M. Barker, *The Gate of Heaven*, op. cit., p. 109.

[163] Wisdom 18: 24.

[164] For a beautiful text in St Ephrem, the saving High Priest saw the fate of Adam and came down to purify him so he could re-enter Paradise. 'The Garden cast him from its midst; all shining it thrust him forth. The High Priest, the Exalted One, beheld him cast from Himself: He stooped down and came to him, He cleansed him with hyssop, and led him back to Paradise.' *Hymns on Paradise* 4, 4. Cited in M. Barker, *The Gate of Heaven*, op. cit., p. 101.

[165] Matthew 17: 1-9, and parallels.

[166] Luke 24: 50-51.

[167] Genesis 14: 48.

[168] Sirach 50: 20. In the light of these texts, the Ascension may be described as 'the high priest entering the holy of holies surrounded with incense': thus M. Barker, *Temple Theology. An Introduction* (London, SPCK, 2004), p. 32. We can compare with this what Barker calls 'the earliest material in the Book of Enoch [which] described how Enoch, a high priestly figure, ascended into a heavenly temple of fire and crystal, in which there was an inner house of fire. The Great Glory sat there on his throne, but none of the angels could enter except Enoch, who was summoned into the presence. This must reflect temple practice, where only the high priest could enter the inner shrine, whilst the other priests were allowed no further than the hall of the temple', ibid., p. 20.

[169] Hebrews 7: 15.

[170] Hebrews 10: 5-7, citing Psalm 40: 7-9.

[171] Hebrews 10: 1-4.

[172] A. Vanhoye, *Old Testament Priests and the New Priest*, op. cit., pp. 208-209. These critical comments are made à propos of J. Smith, *A Priest for Ever. A Study in the Typology and Eschatology of Hebrews* (London and Sydney, Sheed and Ward, 1969).

[173] Ignatius, *To the Philadelphians*, 5.

[174] That is not to say that the present writer can accept the view that the central category in Jesus's self-identification was 'the returning Melchizedek': a 'Barkerian' thesis adopted in L. P. Hemming's remarkable study of the Church's Liturgy in its soteriological and anagogical aspects, *Worship as a Revelation. The Past, Present and Future of Catholic Liturgy* (London, Continuum, 2008).

[175] Psalm 110 (109): 4.

[176] Mark 12: 35-36 and parallels; 14: 62 and parallels. The term 'kingship' was, in the Ancient Near East, somewhat comprehensive and polyvalent compared with later usage. Bentzen prefers the paraphrase 'First Man' for the combined gifts and offices of primordially created man as found in Psalm 8 and Genesis 1: 'This "First Man" is the origin of the functions of king, prophet and priest. In the eschatological "Man" they are again united, in what theologians later called the *munus triplex Christi*', A. Bentzen, *King and Messiah*, op. cit., p. 44.

[177] Either at their coronation, or in connexion with the much-discussed 'New Year' Festival of the enthronement of Yahweh where the king played the part of God's vice-gerent.

[178] I take these examples from David Selbourne's *Moral Evasion* (London, Centre for Policy Studies, 1998), pp. 3-8.

[179] J. Shreeve, 'The Other Stem-Cell Debate', *The New York Times*, 10 April 2005, pp. 41-47.

[180] D. Selbourne, *Moral Evasion*, op. cit., pp. 27-42.

[181] Ibid., pp. 19-24.

[182] J. Sacks, 'Therapy instead of Morality', *The Times*, 5 July 1996.

[183] E. Gilson, *The Spirit of Medieval Philosophy* (English translation, New York, Sheed and Ward, 1940), pp. 352-353.

[184] E. Lucas, *The Life of Frederick Lucas, M.P.* (London, Burns and Oates, 1886), Vol. I., p. 279.

[185] G. K. Chesterton, *The Victorian Age in Literature* (London, Williams and Norgate, 1925), p. 12.

[186] Benedict XVI, 'Ad Romanam Curiam ob omina natalicia', *Acta Apostolicae Sedis* XCVIII (6 January 2006), pp. 40-53.

[187] N. Tanner, 'Chapter V: The Church in the World *(Ecclesia ad extra)*. I. Church and World', in *History of Vatican II, Volume IV: Church as Communion: Third Period and Intersession, September 1964-September 1965*, ed. G. Alberigo, English version ed. J. A. Komonchak (Maryknoll, NY, Orbis, and Leuven, Peeters, 2003), pp. 269-330; G. Routhier, 'Finishing the Work Begun: the Trying Experience of the Fourth Period. IIB. "Schema XII"', in *History of Vatican II, Volume V. The Council and the Transition. The Fourth Period and the End of the Council, September 1965 – December 1965* (Maryknoll, NY, Orbis, and Leuven, Peeters, 2006), pp. 122-177; P. Hünermann, 'The Final Weeks of the Council. III. Final Work on *Gaudium et spes*', ibid., pp. 386-427.

[188] T. Rowland, *Culture and the Thomist Tradition. After Vatican II* (London and New York, Routledge, 2003), especially pp. 11-34.

[189] L. S. Chapp, 'The Retrieval of *Gaudium et Spes*: A Comparison of Rowland and Balthasar', *Nova et Vetera* 3. 1 (2005), pp. 118-146, and here at p. 131.

[190] Ibid., p. 124.

[191] In H. Vorgrimler (ed.), *Commentary on the Documents of Vatican II. V. Pastoral Constitution on the Church in the Modern World* (English translation, New York, Herder, 1969), p. 332.

[192] L. S. Chapp, 'The Retrieval of *Gaudium et Spes*', art. cit.

[193] D. L. Schindler, 'Christology and the *imago Dei*: Interpreting

Gaudium et Spes', *Communio* 23 (1996), pp. 156-184.

[194] D. L. Schindler, *Heart of the Word, Center of the Church. Communio Ecclesiology, Liberalism and Liberation* (Edinburgh, T. and T. Clark, 1996).

[195] Ibid., p. xv.

[196] L. Chapp, 'The Retrieval of *Gaudium et spes'*, art. cit., pp. 128-129.

[197] A. Dulles, 'Orthodoxy and Social Change', *America* 178. 21 (1998), p. 10.

[198] *Christifideles laici*, 37. Thus: for created in God's image and likeness, apart from paragraphs 12 and 22, paragraphs 17 and 21; for redeemed by Jesus Christ, paragraphs 13, 22, 37, 38, and 58; for destined for eternal communion with God, paragraphs 13, 19 and 21.

[199] E. Gilson, *The Spirit of Medieval Philosophy*, op. cit., p. 325.

[200] J. R. R. Tolkien, *The Lord of the Rings* (London, Harper Collins, 2005, 50th Anniversary Edition), pp. 348-349.

[201] R. Scruton, *Sexual Desire. A Philosophical Investigation* (London, Phoenix, 2001).

[202] A. Nichols, O.P., 'Christianity, Secularisation and Islam', *Standpoint* 2 (2008), pp. 44-47. I thank the editor, Daniel Johnson, for permission to re-use some material from this article.

[203] Idem, *The Realm. An Unfashionable Essay on the Conversion of England* (Oxford, Family Publications, 2008).

[204] Ruth 1: 16, 17.

[205] C. Taylor, *A Secular Age* (Harvard, MA, and London, Harvard University Press, 2007), p. 300.

[206] H. L. Dreyfus, 'Nihilism, Art, Technology and Politics', in C. B. Guignon (ed.), *The Cambridge Companion to Heidegger* (Cambridge, Cambridge University Press, 2006, 2nd edition), p. 349.

[207] J. Rist, *Real Ethics. Reconsidering the Foundations of Morality*

(Cambridge, Cambridge University Press, 2002).

[208] D. McShane, 'For Labour, the Scottish Years are Over', *Daily Telegraph*, 27 July 2008.

[209] N. Wolterstorff, *Justice: Rights and Wrongs* (Princeton, NJ, Princeton University Press, 2007).

[210] Benedict XVI, *Deus caritas est*, 28.

[211] The theme of C. Smith, 'Introduction', idem (ed.), *The Secular Revolution: Power, Interests and Conflict in the Secularization of American Public Life* (Berkeley, CA, University of California Press, 2003), pp. 1-96.

[212] G. Olsen, 'The Role of Religion in the Twenty-First Century: A Prolegomenon and Overview', *Communio* 31 (2004), p. 319.

[213] C. Dawson, 'Religion and Mass Civilisation – the Problem of the Future', *Dublin Review* 214.428 (1944), p. 5.

[214] A. MacIntyre, *After Virtue. A Study in Moral Theory* (Notre Dame, IN, Notre Dame University Press, 1984, 2nd edition), pp. 226-236.

[215] G. Olsen, 'The Role of Religion in the Twenty-First Century: A Prolegomenon and Overview', art. cit., pp. 320-321.

[216] 'Englishness, though continually evolving, was very ancient': J. C. D. Clark, 'Protestantism, Nationalism, and National Identity, 1660-1832', *The Historical Journal* 43.1 (2000), p. 262. I am grateful to Professor Clark for the gift of this article, along with that cited in n. 218 below.

[217] P. Wormald, 'Bede, the *Bretwaldas*, and the Origins of the *Gens Anglorum*', in idem, D. Bullough and R. Collins (eds), *Ideal and Reality in Frankish and Anglo-Saxon Society: Studies presented to J. M. Wallace-Hadrill* (Oxford, Blackwell, 1983), pp. 99-129.

[218] J. C. D. Clark, 'The C of E needs a Strong Story', *Church Times*, 31 October 2008, p. 10.

[219] H. de Lubac, S.J., *Catholicisme. Les aspects sociaux du dogme* (Paris, Cerf, 1952, 2nd edition).

[220] M. Cowling, *Religion and Public Doctrine in Modern England. III. Accommodations* (Cambridge, Cambridge University Press, 2001), p. xi.

The Realm

*An Unfashionable Essay
on the Conversion of England*

"Aidan Nichols' small book *The Realm* makes a bold claim about the past and a bold wager about the future . . . Fr Nichols' description of the New Evangelization after Vatican II rings true far beyond Land's End."

– George Weigel

"A radical call for Catholics to stand up and reclaim the intellectual, spiritual and political heritage . . . at the root of everything it means to be English."

– Franz Klein

"Well-argued and convincing."

– Jim Currin

"One of the finest theologians in the English-speaking world."

– Carl Olson

"Some of his assertions hit home hard and true . . . a stimulating book, never dull.

– David Carter

"This is a most important book . . . it is gripping reading."

– Eric Hester

"A man of palpable and infectious vision."

– Jack Carrigan

"The book, for which Catholics, not just in England, but across the UK and Ireland, have been waiting . . . brilliantly argued and bursting full of ideas . . . this could just be the book that every Catholic needs to read this year."

– James Kelly

"Un court et brillant livre."

– Balbino Katz

"Fr Nichols is essentially right: the Church needs a coordinated strategy for drawing individuals to the Catholic faith and transforming English culture from within. His programme is the most convincing yet proposed. We hope his book will inspire English Catholics to think big again."

– Shawn Tribe

"As ever, Fr Nichols gives us a thoughtful and original look at the question of culture. His choice of England as a focus (rather than Britain or the "United Kingdom") is well explained but remains itself one of the provocative aspects of this rewarding book."

– Fr Timothy Finigan

Available from the publishers at www.familypublications.co.uk